D0434324

Safari adventure

Hal and Roger are called in to help when big-game poachers threaten to wipe out the entire population of Tsavo, Africa's largest game reserve.

Using 'dope darts', the boys and their helpers succeed in capturing a band of poachers red-handed, but it takes longer to track down their leader, the mysterious Blackbeard.

While restoring peace to Tsavo, Hal and Roger meet with new and strange experiences – Hal learns to fly an unfamiliar aeroplane in a hurry, and Roger is introduced to the ways of the Masai, a tribe who live only on blood and milk.

Safari Adventure

Willard Price

Illustrated by Pat Marriott

KNIGHT BOOKS
Hodder and Stoughton

Text copyright © 1966 Willard Price

Illustrations copyright © 1966 by Jonathan Cape Ltd

First published by Jonathan Cape Ltd 1966

This edition first published 1970
Fourteenth impression 1985

ISBN 0 340 13500 X

Printed and bound in Great Britain for
Hodder and Stoughton Paperbacks, a
division of Hodder and Stoughton Ltd.,
Mill Road, Dunton Green, Sevenoaks,
Kent (Editorial Office: 47 Bedford
Square, London, WC1 3DP) by Richard Clay
(The Chaucer Press) Ltd.,
Bungay, Suffolk

Contents

1

Poachers' Paradise

THEY were heading for trouble. But Hal, nineteen, was too old to show fear and his brother Roger, thirteen, was too young to realize what he was getting into.

Both felt the tingle of new excitement as the small plane soared above the Mountains of the Moon and pointed its nose east by south-east for Tsavo. Tsavo, home of murder and mystery. Tsavo, Africa's largest national park, where animals should be safe – but were not.

Gangs of poachers were killing the elephants, rhinos, giraffes, hippos, and other wild creatures of Tsavo by the hundred.

What is a poacher? In Africa it means a thief who kills animals without a licence and sells the tusks, horns, or other valuable parts.

Warden Crosby could not stop the killing. He had a force of only ten rangers. How could ten men hope to patrol eight thousand square miles of jungle?

Worry had bitten deep furrows into Mark Crosby's forehead. He sat in the pilot's seat with his hands on the controls, but he paid slight attention to Lake Victoria slipping by below, the source of the Nile, the spot where Stanley met Livingstone, the vast Serengeti lion country, the snow-capped Mount Kilimanjaro. His mind was on the land beyond – the scene of blood, horror, torture, and death.

'It's a war,' he said, 'a war against big odds. We're losing it. We have ten men on our side. Ten men against hundreds of poachers. We no sooner drive them out of one place than they pop up in another. It's pretty hopeless.'

'Have any of your men been killed?' Hal asked.

'We had twenty-two rangers. Twelve have been killed.'

'Poison arrows?'

'Yes, all the poachers are armed – most of them with bows and poison arrows, some with spears and bush knives, some with muskets. Two of our men were caught in traps that the poachers had set out to catch animals.

Those two died a horrible death. We didn't find their skeletons until a month later.'

'Skeletons?'

'That's all that was left of them.'

'I suppose they died of thirst,' said Hal. 'Then the hyenas picked their bones.'

'I doubt if it was that comfortable. Hyenas don't wait till you're dead. They're afraid of you as long as you can fight. But if they find you trapped and helpless, they gang up on you. Those two men were eaten alive.'

Hal winced at the thought of the slow and terrible agony of the two unfortunate rangers. Roger shivered and began to be sorry that he had come.

'Why do you think it was hyenas?' said Hal. 'Why not lions or leopards?'

'A lion is usually a good sport. He seldom attacks unless he is attacked. A leopard isn't such a gentleman. He might attack without provocation. But he has an odd little habit. After he has eaten as much as he can hold, he drags the rest of the carcass up into a tree where it will be safe from other animals until he comes back for another meal. He's very powerful. He could break a body loose from a trap and carry it up even if it was twice his own weight. But nothing like that happened. No, it must have been the work of hyenas. And perhaps vultures. They usually come round after the hyenas have finished and take any scraps that are left.'

Hal and Roger exchanged glances. Their enthusiasm for this adventure had suddenly cooled. They had welcomed Warden Crosby when he had flown to the Mountains of the Moon to get their help. It had seemed a good chance to have a lively adventure, and to save wild animals from death at the hands of the poachers.

Besides, in a way, it was part of their job. Their father, John Hunt, was in the business of collecting wild animals and selling them to zoos where they would have good care and furnish education and entertainment to thousands of spectators. He had taught his sons to love animals and gone with them on their first take-'em-alive journeys. But what would be the use of such journeys if the wild game were all killed off by poachers?

So when the boys and their thirty black helpers had driven out a gang of killers from their hideout in the Mountains of the Moon, Crosby had come to them for aid in his battle against the poachers of Tsavo. They had phoned their father at his animal farm near New York and gained his consent. Now they began to wonder if they had bitten off more than they could chew.

Crosby guessed their thoughts.

'I hope I haven't scared you,' he said.

'Scared us? Of course not,' said Hal stoutly.

'When will your men get here?'

'Well, it's six hundred miles by road. Our jeeps and Land-Rovers aren't built for speed. But they should be here by noon tomorrow.'

'I can't thank you enough for coming in with me on this job.'

'Don't thank us until you see what we can do – if anything.'

'There it is.' Crosby pointed past an elbow of the snow mountain. 'That's Tsavo.'

It was a lovely sight. Who could believe that this beautiful land was a valley of death? It seemed a peaceful paradise of forest and plain, gentle hills, silvery rivers, quiet lakes, bright sun, and dreaming shadow.

Roger, who had a keen appreciation of the beautiful, exclaimed, 'Man! That's cool!'

His older brother said it a little differently. 'Looks like a bit of heaven.'

'It could be just that,' said Crosby, 'if we could get rid of those poachers. It should be a safe refuge for animals and a grand park for visitors. Now it's a death-trap. Do you see that place where the river widens into a sort of lake? We have an underwater observatory there. You can go down into a submarine chamber and look out through port-holes and see crocodiles swimming under water and hippos walking on the bottom. But recently the poachers slaughtered dozens of the hippos and all you could see through the port-holes was a huge heap of rotting corpses. The decaying carcasses polluted the river, and the smell was terrible. Some hippo babies left alive were nudging their dead mothers and dying of starvation. But they didn't suffer long – the crocodiles snapped them up.'

'What good did it do the poachers to kill the hippos and then leave them to rot?' asked Hal.

'Oh, but they got what they wanted. They took the heads – each of them would be worth a couple of thousand dollars. And strips of the hide had been cut off.'

'What could they do with them?'

'Make whips. The hide is very thick. They dry the strips in the shade for several weeks. It becomes as hard as a board. Then each strip is sawed, like wood, into rods about three feet long. These can be used as canes.

But generally they are shipped to South Africa where the Boers trim the edges to make them sharp and use them as whips, called *sjamboks*. A sjambok will cut the flesh like a knife. Cattle are afraid of it, and men too. You don't pick a quarrel with your boss if he's armed with a sjambok. Many a man has been killed by a hippo whip.'

'It all sounds pretty cruel to me,' Hal said, 'murdering a hippo to make a murder weapon.'

'It's a beastly business. And a *big* business. Of course poaching is as old as history. But it has always been a small business – until now. A native who needed meat might go out and kill an antelope. But now it's organized on a big scale. What they're after now is not just some meat for supper, but millions of dollars, and instead of a lone poacher here or there we now have armies of poachers directed by a man they call Blackbeard – because of his black beard and because he's a pirate like the original Blackbeard, only he steals tusks and tails, horns and hides, instead of gold. And he's guilty of more torture and killing than the first Blackbeard ever was.'

'Who is this Blackbeard?'

'I wish I knew. He's a man of mystery. I don't believe he's a native. We've done a lot of guessing but we get nowhere. Perhaps you can solve the mystery. We've wondered if he might be a big merchant down in Mombasa, the port city. We know great quantities of hippo heads, elephant tusks, rhino horns, valuable skins of leopards, cheetahs, monkeys, pythons, and all that are shipped out from Mombasa to cities all over the world. Somebody is making a fortune out of this racket. Perhaps he's *not* a merchant. Perhaps he's a military man who knows how to rule this army of poachers. Just guesses. We really have no idea who he is. Until he's caught, this thing will probably go on.'

2

Poisoned arrows

THE plane was now gliding down towards the troubled paradise. It was a Stork – a German-made four-seater. It had dual controls – one joystick was gripped by the pilot and Hal, sitting in the co-pilot's seat, watched the other stick moving restlessly in front of him.

He longed to get his hands on it. But he wasn't sure that he could fly this crate. He had flown his father's Navion over Long Island, but that was a quite different machine. Here, every dial on the instrument board seemed to be in the wrong place. And everything was in metres and kilometres and Centigrade and European symbols, and words were in German.

Besides, every plane handles differently. One will be as steady as a cart-horse, another as skittish as a bucking bronco. He hoped that some time he would be allowed to pilot the plane, but first he must have full instructions and plenty of practice with Crosby at his side.

'That sharp-pointed hill with the pavilion on top,' said Crosby, 'is called Poachers' Lookout. A telescope is mounted in front of the pavilion. We keep a ranger there all day, every day, watching for poachers.'

'How far can you see from that point?'

'Not far enough. You can spot anything within a few miles but then the hills and forests cut off the view. It would take at least a hundred such lookouts to cover our eight thousand miles of territory, and that would mean a hundred watchers. Of course that's impossible. So we do what we can with this movable lookout.'

'You mean this plane?'

'Yes. But I'm the only one who can fly it. And I can't be in the air all the time – I have other things to do. When I locate some poachers I fly back to camp, get together any rangers who are not out on duty and we drive in a Land-Rover to the place where I have seen the poachers. If there are only one or two, we may be able to arrest them. But if it turns out to be a gang, we're lucky if we can get back to camp with only one or two dead rangers. Now you can see our camp – just beyond Poachers' Lookout.'

Hal could make out a cluster of thatch-roofed cabins above five miles ahead. So this was the famous Kitani Safari Lodge where visitors from Europe and America might spend a few days enjoying the thrilling experience of being completely surrounded by wild animals. He was surprised to see that there was no wall or fence around the camp.

'How do you keep the animals out?'

Crosby laughed. 'We don't. We could never afford to build a wall strong enough or high enough. Leopards or lions could scramble over the top of it. Elephants can push down big trees – they could push down a wall. Rhinos are irritated by anything that gets in their way –

they would charge a wall and drive a hole straight through it. Buffaloes have heads as hard as battering rams. They smash heavy trucks and lorries. A stampede of buffaloes would make short work of a wall if they took a notion to see what was on the other side. No, a wall wouldn't be practical, and as for a fence, it would be trampled down in one night.'

'So you let the animals come right into the camp?'

'Right. They seldom come in during the day. But every night we have visitors. We advise our guests not to go walking in the moonlight, but stay in their cabins after sunset. And keep their windows closed - leopards like to climb in. Elephants come looking for water. One wily old rascal has learned how to turn on the taps in the garden - but doesn't bother to turn them off again. He drinks his fill and wanders off and I have to go out and turn off the tap.'

Roger's sharp eyes had been scanning the landscape.

'Speaking of fences,' he said, 'that looks like one over there - on the left. What could that be?'

The warden took one look, then swung the plane about and headed for the thing that looked like a fence.

'Nothing the matter with your eyes,' he said to Roger. 'You'd make a good ranger. That's a trap-line.'

'Trap-line?'

'A line of traps set by the poachers.'

'But it looks like a fence or a hedge.'

'Exactly. The poachers pile up thorn bushes to make a fence. This one appears to be about a mile long. But you notice there are gaps in the fence. In every one of those openings they put a trap.'

'What's the idea?'

'Well, suppose you were an animal. You come up to this fence and you want to get to the other side. It's too wide to jump over. You don't wish to plough through it because you know you'd get stuck by thousands of thorns, sharp as needles, each one about three inches long. So you run beside the fence hoping to find a way to get through. You come to one of these gaps. You dash in and suddenly find yourself in trouble. Your head passes through a wire noose that tightens round your neck. The more you pull the tighter it gets. You struggle and twist and the wire cuts deeper and deeper into your throat and the blood attracts the carnivores which proceed to eat you alive.'

'But if I am eaten, then the poachers don't get anything.'

'Oh yes they do. If you are an elephant, the chances are all they want is your tusks, or perhaps your feet to make waste-paper baskets, or your tail to be sold as a fly switch. The wild beasts don't eat those parts. So the beast gets its dinner and the poacher gets the rest and they are both satisfied.'

They were now dropping fast towards the thorn hedge.

'What do you plan to do?' Hal inquired.

'Just give the poachers a good scare. Let them know that their camp has been located. Sometimes that's enough to make them pack up and leave. Of course, it may not work. There may be a lot of them and they know we have very few rangers. But they don't know that tomorrow we are going to have thirty more men - your men. We'll come out here tomorrow by road, the whole lot of us, and give them the surprise of their lives.

Now I'm going to give you a good look at this trap-line.'

The plane swooped lower. The beginning of the hedge was directly underneath. Looking down the line, the boys could see that almost every gap held an animal. Some hung still and lifeless. Some struggled fiercely and their screams could be heard over the roar of the engine. Packs of hyenas, jackals, wild dogs, and other meat-eaters were enjoying a feast. The strange 'laugh' of the hyenas, the yapping of the wild dogs, the yipping of the jackals, the occasional rumble of a leopard or roar of a lion added to the general tumult.

So that the boys could get a good look, the warden had cut the motor down to about thirty miles per hour. The Stork, with its flaps down, was quite capable of staying in the air at this slow speed, though its normal speed was one hundred and forty.

Now the temporary straw shacks of the poachers could be seen among the trees. Crosby, flying within fifty feet of the ground, examined the camp closely. 'Bigger than I thought,' he said.

Suddenly a swarm of black figures burst out of the forest, armed with bows and spears. A volley of spears and arrows came climbing towards the little plane.

If this were an ordinary plane, they would harmlessly pepper the bottom of the fuselage. But the cabin of the Stork is enclosed in a bubble of Perspex, which even curves in a little at the bottom towards the floorboards, so that the occupants of the plane can look straight down to the ground beneath. This is ideal for the purpose of complete visibility but offers little protection against ground fire.

Since Crosby was gripping the control, his elbow was

well out in the bulge of Perspex. Suddenly he jerked it in
with a little exclamation of surprise. He dropped the exposed arm beside him where Hal would not see it and
held the stick with his other hand. Sharply he gunned the
plane up well out of reach of ground fire, then levelled
off straight for Kitani Safari Lodge.

3

Race with death

HAL was unaware of what had happened. But Roger, sitting behind the warden, saw the black arrow that had gone through Crosby's arm just above the elbow. The arrow-head had passed through the fleshy part of the arm and come out on the other side.

'Hal, look,' Roger said. 'The warden – his arm . . .'

Hal leaned forward so that he could see the half-hidden arm and arrow.

'Never mind it now,' Crosby said. 'The important thing is to get you to camp before I go to sleep.'

'You think the arrow was poisoned?'

'Probably.'

Hal examined the arrow-head, looking for the black, gummy paste made from the highly poisonous Acocanthera plant.

'I don't see anything – except your own blood.'

'You wouldn't see anything on the point. They don't put the poison there.'

'Why not?'

'Because they might prick themselves with it. A man tumbling around in the bush with a quiverful of arrows on his back with all the poisoned tips sticking up would be a great danger to himself and to his friends.'

'Then where do they put the poison?'

'On the shaft, just behind the arrow-head.'

'But that's the part that's in your arm. Shouldn't we get it out of there as quickly as we can?'

'You can't reach it.' It was true. The front seats were almost two feet apart. The injured arm was on the warden's far side. Hal could not get at it without interfering with the control of the plane.

'I can reach it,' Roger said. 'Just tell me what to do.'

Hal thought a moment. The arrow-head was barbed. 'You can't pull it back,' he said. 'Try to break off the arrow-head. Then pull out the shaft.'

Roger leaned over the back of the pilot's seat, gripped the arrow-head and did his best to snap it off. The wood was very tough. He put on more pressure. His hand was wet with blood. Sweat came out on his face and he felt faint – not that the effort hurt him, but he knew he was hurting the warden. Crosby said not a word.

Crack – the barbed head broke off.

Now for the most painful part of the operation. Roger hoped to make his patient suffer as little as possible. One good jerk and he would get the shaft out of the arm.

He laid hold with both hands, gritted his teeth, and gave one mighty tug. The shaft held fast. The plane staggered. Crosby at once brought it back under control.

'Must be wedged between muscle and bone,' Hal said. 'Give it another try.'

Roger had once thought he would like to be a surgeon. Now he changed his mind. His body was streaming with sweat and it wasn't because this country, Kenya, is

crossed by the equator. He knew the agony he was caus-
ing. He laid his bloody hands on the shaft again, gathered
up all his strength and yanked. No luck.

He worked the shaft up and down to enlarge the hole.
He knew this must hurt like the devil, but he didn't
know what else to do. Once more he yanked and the
shaft came free.

The warden opened his mouth, and Roger expected
him to shout something like, 'You clumsy kid!' but all
he said was, 'Good boy!'

'Give me that,' Hal said. He took the shaft and looked
at the part that had been embedded in the flesh. Through
the blood he could see a black sticky substance.

'I'm afraid that's it,' he said.

What chance did the warden have? He might live, he
might die. Hal had seen Africans preparing this stuff.
They themselves were deathly afraid of it. They took
great care not to get a bit of it on themselves. They
boiled it out in the bush, not in the village – that would
be too dangerous. A drop might spatter out of the pot on
to the skin of a man, woman, or child. If there was a
scratch on the skin, even though it might be no larger
than a pin point, the poison would enter.

What happened then would depend upon the strength
of the poison and the physical endurance of the person
who was poisoned. A child might die in a few minutes.
One woman died while she was being carried a few hundred feet to her house. Another died within twenty
minutes. Hal had heard of a man who lasted three hours
before he died. A strong man who had been struck by
the arrow of an enemy tribe lay unconscious for two
hours and then recovered.

It made a difference whether the poison was fresh or stale. If it was new it acted quickly. If it had been on the arrow-shaft for many days and had dried and been covered with dust it might not cause death.

The warden slumped against the stick, pushing it forward. Immediately the plane plunged towards the earth in a steep spiral.

Hal seized the stick in front of him and tried to pull it back. He couldn't do it – Crosby's weight against the other control was too much.

The earth was approaching at terrifying speed. 'Pull him up,' Hal shouted to Roger.

Roger had plenty to do to hold himself up in this crazy contraption whirling on its nose like a top. His seat-belt helped a little. He supported himself against the back of the front seat with one arm, got his other arm around the warden's neck and heaved. Crosby was not a light man and if Roger had not been big for his years he could not have budged the heavy body. He raised it a few inches, then a few inches more, and, with Hal pulling on the control at the same time, the plane hesitated in its dizzy dive and began to point upwards.

A few more head-over-heels revolutions and the wings steadied, the whirling stopped and the plane swooped upwards just in time to escape the reaching arms of a tall kapok tree.

Roger still held back the warden's unconscious body while Hal settled down to the uneasy business of flying a strange plane without either practice or instructions. He had to guess his way across the instrument board and some of his guesses were pretty wild.

Where was the gizmo that controlled the brakes? Or

were they governed by the foot pedals? The most tick-
lish job would be landing. He must get ready for it. How
did you lower the flaps? Any one of half a dozen levers
might do it. He tried them until he found one that pro-
duced the right effect – the sudden check of extra lift and
drag.

Once on the ground, he must apply the brake so that
he wouldn't taxi right off the strip into a tree or a cabin.
How to do that he couldn't tell until he was actually on
the ground. Then it might be too late.

Meanwhile he peered ahead through the whirling pro-
peller, looking for the landing field. His eye travelled all
round the thatch buildings of the safari camp without
finding an asphalt runway.

Finally he spotted a wind-sock. That must mark the
airstrip, but where was the strip? The landing field
appeared to be just that and nothing more – a field.

He was now directly over the camp. He circled the
field, calculating the chances of getting down to it without striking the trees that blocked it at each end.

He was just about to come in for a landing when he
saw something peculiar in the middle of the field. Something yellow and black lay on the green grass. Then a
part of it moved and he knew what it was: a family of
lions.

They were basking in the sun, quite undisturbed by
the noisy plane. Hal knew that lions were not afraid of
planes, trains, or cars. More than once he had driven his
Land-Rover close to a pride of lions and stopped within
fifteen feet of them and they did not budge an inch.
Kings of the animal world, they were not easily
frightened.

He could not wait for them to wander off. They might not move for an hour or more. He had a patient on board who required prompt attention. He had to get rid of those lions, and fast.

He swooped down to within twenty feet of them. They were all stretched out comfortably in the grass. Some looked up at him lazily, others did not even open their

eyes. One huge black-maned male lay on his back with all four paws in the air. He did not even bother to roll over.

Hal circled and came in again, lower this time. He kept the throttle full open in order to make as much thunder as possible. It was a dangerous business, roaring in at a hundred and forty miles per hour so close to the ground. This time one lioness with a brood of cubs decided they would be safer on the sidelines and led them away.

Encouraged by this success, Hal made another dive. This time he would really singe the fur of these haughty beasts.

He didn't quite do that, but he came so close that when he circled up again he saw that the lions were on their feet, the males roaring angrily, and even the upside-down animal had taken notice of this buzzing gadfly that was disturbing his slumbers. The whole pride moved away with slow dignity to the edge of the field.

Hal at once lowered his flaps, throttled down to a glide and came in for a more or less perfect landing. The brake linkage seemed to be as he had hoped, and he brought the plane to a bumpy halt within a few feet of the trees.

4

The judge

THE warden seemed dead to the world. Hal felt his pulse.
The heart was beating, though faintly. So there was still
a chance.

The helpless body was eased down to the ground. A
man came running from the camp. He was dressed
smartly in a light-coloured uniform that ended at his
elbows and his knees and contrasted with his very black
skin. His military-looking cap had an insignia in front
and a thin cloth kepi behind hanging down over the back
of his neck to keep off insects, after the fashion of the old-
time French Foreign Legion. This must be one of the
warden's ten rangers.

'What happen?' he asked, stooping beside the body in
the grass.

'Poison arrow,' Hal said.

The ranger put his ear to the warden's chest.

'No dead. We take to the judge. Judge, he fix.'

'He needs a doctor.'

'No doctor. Judge, he good, he fix.'

Hal didn't wait to ask questions about the judge who
could fix. There was one thing that could be done at

once. He whipped out a handkerchief and tied it round the arm above the bleeding wound.

Together, they carried the warden to the main building. The interior was furnished with comfortable chairs and a large desk. It evidently served the warden as both home and office. The unconscious warden was carried into his bedroom and laid on the bed. A little man came bustling into the room.

'This is the judge,' said the ranger. 'He fix.'

The judge's slightly dark skin marked him as a native of India. There were many Indians in Kenya.

'An accident?' he said.

Hal explained briefly what had happened.

'Ah yes,' said the little judge. 'How fortunate that I was here. I know exactly what to do.'

Roger, whose eyes had a way of seeing things that other people did not notice, saw the bright light that came into the judge's eyes. The judge seemed almost happy. Perhaps it was just his kindly nature. Perhaps he was happy because he could help.

'First,' he said, 'off with that tourniquet.' He quickly untied it and flung it aside.

'But I just put it on,' said Hal. 'I wanted to stop the poison from going through his system.'

'You meant well,' said the judge kindly. 'But, you see, it's better to allow the poison to be diffused through the entire system than concentrated in one spot.'

Hal had never heard this theory before, but it sounded logical.

'Shouldn't the wound be syringed with distilled water?' Hal asked.

'Wrong again, my boy.' The judge spoke like a father

gently reproving his foolish son. 'What he needs is an injection.'

'Ammonium carbonate?' asked Hal.

The judge's eyes narrowed. He seemed surprised that Hal should know these things, and a little annoyed. He covered his annoyance with a sweet smile.

'Yes, yes,' he replied. 'I'll see if there is any in the dispensary.'

He left the room, walked across the lounge and into another room. Hal quietly followed him. He arrived just in time to see the judge pick up a bottle from the front row and put it back behind everything else on the shelf so that it could not easily be seen.

He turned and saw Hal. 'No Ammonium here,' he said. 'Never mind. I know something better. Coramine. A heart stimulant. That's what he needs – something to keep his heart going.'

Hal agreed. His confidence in the little judge was restored. He helped him search the shelves for Coramine.

'Hal!' Roger called. 'Come quick!' Hal ran to the bedroom. 'I think he's stopped breathing,' Roger said.

The warden was as pale as paper. Beads of sweat stood out on his skin. Hal put his mouth to the warden's and breathed, slowly, powerfully, forcing air in, drawing it out, forcing it in, drawing it out, forcing it in, drawing it out.

He kept it up until the patient breathed again. But the breathing would die out once more if the heart didn't get a boost. Where was the judge with that Coramine?

The judge came in holding a hypodermic syringe. He inserted it into the wound. That was a strange place to put it. Wouldn't the thigh be better? Then Hal noticed

that the liquid in the syringe was a blackish brown.

In a sudden panic he seized the syringe and drew it out before the judge could press the plunger. The judge stared at him with astonishment.

'Pardon me,' Hal said, 'but isn't there some mistake? That doesn't look like Coramine. It looks like Acocanthera.'

The judge gazed at the syringe. 'I do believe you're right,' he said. 'I am happy that you noticed it. I know now how it happened. The two bottles were side by side and I got the wrong one.'

Hal was already on his way to the dispensary and the judge followed. Hal was suspicious, but his suspicion faded when he saw that it was just as the judge had said.

The two bottles, one labelled 'Coramine' and the other labelled 'Aco', the safari man's nickname for the deadly Acocanthera, really did stand side by side. That was natural, for they were frequently used one after the other. When it was necessary to capture a large animal such as a rhino or elephant, a ranger might puncture the skin with a very light touch of Aco, enough to put the animal to sleep but not enough to kill it, and after the beast was caged it could be revived with an injection of Coramine.

Dismissing his unkind suspicions, Hal helped the judge find a clean syringe and fill it with Coramine.

'Permit me,' Hal said, and himself took the syringe to the bedroom and injected the contents into the patient's thigh.

For half an hour he kept his fingers on the pulse. At first the heart-beat was so faint he could hardly feel it. Then it broke into a rapid palpitation. That was not a very good sign. But it finally settled down to a normal beat that slowly gained in strength.

All this time the judge was pacing up and down the room with every appearance of anxiety.

'A very fine man, the warden,' he said. 'We couldn't afford to lose him. We need him to help save our poor dear animals from the hands of the poachers. It's a cause very close to my heart. In fact I am one of the directors of the African Wildlife Society. Really, the tortures these poor beasts undergo would make you weep. No punishment is enough for those atrocious poachers. Of course as a judge I get them through my court – when they come before me you can be sure they will suffer for their crimes.'

Tears stood in the little judge's eyes as he looked at the helpless body of the warden.

'We are like brothers, the warden and I. If he should die it would break my heart.' He dabbed at his eyes with his handkerchief.

Hal thought, He's either a sweet soul or a great actor. Always willing to believe the best of anyone, he decided that the judge was a sweet soul.

But Roger was looking at the judge with his face screwed up as if he smelt something bad.

5

Friend or enemy?

THE patient stirred. The judge rushed to his side. 'I'll take over,' he said. Hal stepped back and the judge took his place, his fingers on the warden's pulse.

So when the warden opened his eyes the first thing he saw was the anxious, tear-stained face of the sweet soul. And the first thing he felt was the pressure of the judge's warm hand upon his wrist.

He lay quiet for some time. When he did speak his weak voice gave some idea of the ordeal his strong body had suffered.

'Thank you, judge,' he said. 'I can always depend upon you.' Then he noticed the boys. 'You have met?'

'Not exactly,' the judge said. 'We were too concerned about you to take time to introduce ourselves.'

'Then shake hands with Hal Hunt. And his brother Roger. Boys, meet Judge Sindar Singh, my dearest friend. This is not the first time he has saved my life. However did you do it, Sindar?'

'It was nothing, my friend,' Judge Singh replied in his softest, smoothest voice. 'Just a matter of knowing what to do. Coramine and all that.'

'The judge is a very modest man,' Crosby said to the boys. 'I hope you watched him closely so that you'll know what to do if you ever have a case of poisoning to deal with.'

'Yes,' Hal said. 'We watched him closely.'

It was on the tip of his tongue to add, 'If we hadn't watched him closely, you would be dead now.' But he didn't say it. After all, anyone could have made that mistake – getting the wrong dope in the syringe. It *must* have been a mistake. What possible reason could the pleasant little judge have for wanting to kill the warden?

Of course if anyone really wanted to commit murder that was a perfect way to do it. There was already Aco in the wound. If more were injected in the same place, no one would be able to tell, even in an autopsy, that it had not come from the arrow. Hal brushed away the evil thought. The beaming smiles of the little judge over the patient's recovery were strong evidence of his devotion to his friend.

'You'll be glad to know, Sindar,' – the warden's voice was stronger now – 'that the boys are going to help us round up the poachers.'

'Very nice,' smiled the judge. 'But, with all due respect, I'm afraid two boys won't get far against those gangs of killers.'

'Ordinary boys would not. But these are not quite ordinary. They've already had a lot of experience. Their father is a famous animal collector and he has taught them how to get along in rough country. They've taken animals alive, even the big ones – don't you remember reading in the papers about their capture of the fifty-thousand-dollar white elephant in the Mountains of the Moon?'

'But catching an animal is a bit different from a war on poachers,' suggested the judge mildly.

'They've had a taste of that sort of thing too. Anyhow, they'll have thirty men to help them – they're on the road now.'

'When do they arrive?'

'Tomorrow at midday.'

The news seemed to electrify the little judge.

'Well, well, I must be going. I just dropped in to see you on my way to Nairobi. I must move along or I won't get there before night. Take care of yourself, Mark. Sorry you picked up that arrow. Where did you say the gang is operating?'

'I didn't say. Their camp is due west, about seven miles.'

'Good luck with your raid. I do wish I could be with you but I'll be pretty busy tomorrow. Glad to have met you, boys. Watch your step. Remember, this isn't Long Island.' He gave them a sweet smile, and was gone.

'You boys have had quite a day,' Crosby said. 'You'd probably like to rest. Don't bother any more about me – I'll be all right. Your banda is Number Three. It's unlocked. Just move in and make yourselves at home. If there's anything you want, ask a ranger.'

As the boys left the building they saw a car driving away. It must be Judge Singh's.

But there was something wrong. The car was not heading north on to the Nairobi road. It was going west.

They squinted into the descending sun and watched until the car disappeared down the forest trail. Roger said uneasily, 'There's something a little fishy about everything that guy does.'

The banda – to use the African name for a cabin or cottage – was very comfortable. In fact, to the boys, who had been living in a tent during their adventures in the Mountains of the Moon, it seemed luxurious. It had a large living-room with big chairs. You could sit back and look up at the inside of the thatch roof where lizards clung upside down and every now and then pounced upon a fly. There was a small bedroom with two beds, a large bath, a pantry, and, best of all, a broad porch with camp chairs and a dining-table.

The kitchen was a separate small building about thirty feet behind the banda. A native boy came running from it to ask what they would like to have for dinner.

It was pleasant, having dinner in the open, looking out to the panorama of hill and valley and distant blue mountains. Highest of the peaks was Kilimanjaro, 19,000 feet, taller than anything else in the entire continent of Africa, topped with snow and glaciers.

'It looks like the Matterhorn,' Roger said.

'Yes. But it's about a mile higher than the Matterhorn.'

'Bet it's cold up there.'

'To go from here to the top would be like travelling from the equator to Iceland – there'd be that much change in climate.'

'Has anybody ever been to the top?'

'Oh yes. It's not so hard to climb – on the other side. But on this side it had everybody buffaloed until 1964.'

'I don't wonder. It looks as steep as a wall. Who climbed it?'

'Two Royal Air Force men. It took them fifty hours – one way. A little over two days and nights. They went right up the face of the wall, clinging like flies, watching every foothold and fingerhold. They slept standing up – wedged into small clefts and tied to steel pegs driven into the rock. One of them had a nightmare – he struggled, and pulled the pegs loose. He woke just in time to save himself from falling five thousand feet straight down.'

The sun had now left the valley of death but still glorified the snowy heights of Kilimanjaro. The white had changed to a warm pink and, as the sun sank lower, the pink snow turned blood-red which gradually became black under a canopy of brilliant stars.

The animals that dared to visit the camp at night began to arrive. The grass around the bandas was kept watered, and attracted grass-eating animals. There was a distinct chomping, chewing sound. Straining their eyes, the boys could dimly make out stripes.

Hal brought out the binoculars and looked in the direction of the sound. It was remarkable how much better one could see with these things, even at night.

'Zebras,' he said. 'A whole herd of them.'

'What's the other noise?' Roger said. 'Sounds like water.' He took the glasses. As he put them to his eyes, a monster loomed in front of him. It seemed so close that he could almost touch it. 'It's an elephant,' he said. 'He's turning on a tap.'

'Come off it,' said Hal. 'That was just a story.'

'No, it's true. Look for yourself.'

Through the binoculars Hal could darkly see the huge

beast actually turning the tap with the finger-like points at the end of his trunk. The dribble of water from the tap became a rushing stream. The elephant curved his trunk beneath the tap to catch the water. Then he threw back his head, opened his cavernous mouth, lifted his trunk, and threw the water down his throat. He repeated this act over and over again. Hal estimated that he put away five or six gallons.

But after he had finished drinking he was not done with the water. He tossed trunkfuls of it back over his

body to wash off the jungle dust. When he had given himself a thoroughly good bath he grunted with pleasure, turned round, and ambled off into the darkness, leaving the tap still running.

'We'd better turn that thing off,' Hal said. 'If we don't the warden will – and he shouldn't get out of bed.'

'Isn't it dangerous?' Roger said. 'You don't know what else might be sneaking round that tap.'

'Nonsense. You scare too easily.'

'Oh, is that so? And I suppose you're not one bit afraid. Then why don't you turn it off?'

'All right, I will. Just to show you what a fraidy cat you are.'

Hal stepped off the porch on to the grass. He couldn't see so well without the binoculars. He could go back into the banda and get his torch – but why bother ? He could tell by the sound where the tap was.

He didn't know that his mischief-loving brother had stepped off the porch on the other side and was circling round him.

Stepping carefully, Hal picked his way across the lawn to the tap, fumbled for the valve, and turned it off. He had no sooner begun the return journey to the porch than he was startled by the roar of a wild beast close behind him. It sent ripples of fear up and down his backbone. He leaped like an antelope back to the safety of the porch, his one instinct to get inside that banda and close the door. But he must pick up his brother first. He groped where Roger had been, but Roger was not there. Well, he must have heard the beast and gone inside. Hal lost no time in shutting the door between him and the angry animal.

'Roger,' he said, 'you here?'

No answer.

'Roger, where are you?'

An animal-like laugh came from the porch. A laughing hyena? No, it was that infernal brother of his.

'You young rascal, come in here.'

Roger came in, still laughing. Hal couldn't help laughing too. 'So it was you all the time, you scamp.' But he wasn't going to let the kid off so easily. He grabbed Roger, backed into a chair, and tried to bend the boy over his knee for a good spanking. He used to be able to do that – but now Roger was too strong for him.

Roger twisted himself off the spanker's lap and overturned Hal's chair so that he went sprawling on his back, surprising a rat that scampered away squeaking with alarm.

'All right, young man,' Hal laughed, picking himself up. 'That's enough for now. I'll get you later. Just now I'm going to bed. We have a big day tomorrow.'

When they were ready for bed, Roger sniffed the air.

'It's stuffy in here. Smells ratty. Don't you think we ought to have a window open?'

'The warden said no. A leopard might climb in.'

'I think he was just playing it safe when he said that. It's not really very likely, is it?'

'I wouldn't take a chance on it.'

'How about this small window over my bed?' Roger suggested.

'A leopard could get through it.'

'It's too high from the ground.'

'You'd be surprised how high a leopard can jump.'

Roger lay quiet for a moment. Another rat – or was it

the same one? – scuttled across the floor.

'I don't like the smell of this place,' announced Roger. 'I'm going to open that window.'

Hal answered sleepily, 'Okay, you young idiot, open it. But don't be surprised if you have a visitor.'

Roger opened the window, then flopped down under the covers and went to sleep.

6

Leopard comes to call

HE dreamed that he was tussling with his brother. Hal sat on him, squeezing the breath out of him.

He woke with a start. Something *was* on top of him. A leopard? He was about to scream and wrench himself free when another thought came to him.

Hal had said he would get him later. He had scared Hal out of his wits by pretending to be a wild beast about to spring upon his back. Now Hal was trying to scare him – make him think that a leopard had pounced on him. He would fool the big boob. He'd just lie there as calm as you please.

'Ho, ho, hi, hum,' he yawned. 'Go back to bed, you big stiff. You're not fooling me a bit.'

He felt hot breath on his face. Sharp points like claws pressed through the blanket on to his arms.

'You ought to cut your fingernails,' he said.

The answer was a roar that sounded like a circular saw going through a knot.

Roger laughed. 'Pretty poor imitation of a leopard. Now get off me – I want to sleep.'

'What's going on over there?' came from the other side of the room.

Roger's blood froze. 'Where are you, Hal?' he quavered.

'In bed, of course. Something woke me up. Sounded like a leopard.'

There was a scampering sound on the floor. Whatever it was that had landed on Roger leaped off and went careering madly round the room. Hal dug under his pillow for his flashlight and turned it on. Roger saw spots before his eyes – black spots on yellow chasing a big rat.

The leopard caught the rat, gripped it between his teeth, jumped on Roger, squeezing out of that terrified boy one wild yell, then leaped out of the window.

Roger found himself shivering and sweating at the same time. Hal got out of bed and came over.

'Have you had enough fresh air?' he asked. He closed the window. Without saying anything more, he sat down on the edge of the bed, put his hand on Roger's arm and kept it there until the shivering died down. Then, with a final friendly pat, he went back to bed.

Roger lay listening to the sounds of the night. The animals had really taken over the camp. He recognized some of the sounds – the whine of a jackal, the hoot of an owl, and the familiar 'ugh-ugh' of the animal he had come to know so well, most numerous of all four-legged creatures in the East African animal land – the gnu or wildebeest.

There was the 'meow' that sounded like the voice of a house cat but came more probably from a beast twenty times as big, the cheetah. A rhino snorted like a car backfiring. There was a great clatter as the rubbish bin beside the kitchen went over. That might be the work of hyenas. He was more sure of it when he heard a loud chorus of laughter from those weird beasts – 'tee-hee-hee-hee-hee-ha-ha'. From the distant river came an answering laugh from the hippos, a deep sound, 'wah-wah-wah', and, deeper still, 'hoh-hoh-hoh-hoh'.

And for every sound he knew there were a dozen he did not know. He enjoyed listening to them – until he heard one he knew too well – the leopard's saw going through a hard knot.

He buried one ear in his pillow, covered the other with his blanket, and slept.

It seemed only five minutes later when he was aroused by a knock on the door. He opened his eyes to the grey light of dawn.

The door opened and the warden, Mark Crosby, came in.

'You boys want to go on dawn patrol? It's the best time of day to see the animals.'

The boys were surprised to see the warden on his feet. He must have a strong constitution. 'How's your arm?' Hal asked. He saw the arm was bandaged.

'Not bad at all,' the warden said. 'See, I can move it. I was lucky that the arrow just went through the fleshy part. A few days in a bandage and it will be okay. Pull on your clothes and we'll have some coffee.'

When they came out on to the porch they found the boy had already placed a coffee pot and cups on the table. Morning mists were rising. The lower part of Kilimanjaro could not be seen but the snow-crowned top rising above the mists floated like a white cloud in the sky. The sun had already struck the snow and glaciers.

Here below it was still so dark that the shapes moving among the flat-topped acacia trees looked more like blobs of ink than animals.

Crosby saw Roger looking towards the kitchen as if he expected more than coffee. The warden laughed.

'Our ways may seem a little odd to you. The animals are out in full force in the early morning, so we get our guests up at dawn and take them out to see the wild life, then bring them back at about nine for breakfast.'

'Speaking of guests,' said Hal, 'none of these other bandas seems to be occupied.'

Crosby shook his head. 'Very few tourists come here, now that the park has been overrun by killers. Tourists are afraid to come. That's one of the serious effects of poaching. It scares off visitors. And that means it scares off money that this young nation of Kenya needs. The country's biggest source of revenue has been the tourist business. Without the money the tourists bring in, the country will go broke. So if we can get rid of the poachers we'll not only save the animals – we'll save Kenya.'

They climbed into the warden's Land-Rover and set out. They had not gone more than half a mile before the trail was blocked by a herd of buffalo. Almost a hundred of the great shaggy black beasts faced them, with heads lowered. Crosby stopped the car.

'I don't think we'll try to plough through that,' he said.

A huge bull buffalo came out from the herd, advanced some twenty feet towards the Land-Rover and then stopped. He glared at the car and shook his big head.

'That's their leader,' Crosby said. 'If he takes a notion to charge us, they'll all follow.'

'Will they go round the car?'

'Buffaloes don't go round anything. They go through it. Many hunters claim they are the most dangerous animals in Africa. They stop at nothing. Their heads are like iron balls. After they had finished there would be nothing left of this car but scrap iron.'

'And they have the bad habit of coming back,' said Hal, remembering his own adventures with these determined beasts.

'Yes,' said Crosby. 'Most animals do what damage they can and then call it a day. But the buffalo comes back to make sure that you are good and dead. Of course they aren't always dangerous. If nothing annoys them they may be as quiet as cows. That's why we're just sitting here, doing nothing. If they get it through their thick noddles that we mean no harm, they may wander off. It all depends on the poachers.'

'What have the poachers to do with it?'

'If a poacher's arrow or spear has ever wounded that bull, he will hate everything human and he will very likely take it out on us. But I think I recognize him by that twisted right horn. I believe he's been round the camp and I gave him a drink. Let's see if he knows me.'

He opened the door and prepared to climb out. At once there was an angry roar from the big bull. The herd behind him began to stamp and bellow. The bull started forward and Hal longed to get his hands on the gear lever and back away.

But as the warden stepped down to where the bull could see him from head to foot the bull stopped and appeared to be thinking things over.

Then he turned towards the herd and said something that might have been bull-language for 'This two-legged one is okay.' With great dignity he moved off into the woods and the herd followed him.

Hal and Roger breathed again.

'Next stop, Poachers' Lookout,' said the warden as he climbed back behind the wheel.

They drove through some pleasant woodland where they saw long-faced hartebeest, waterbuck, gerenuk, and the lovely, leaping impala, expert in both the high jump and the long jump. The clown of the woods, the wart-hog, humph-humphed out of their way, and a family of baboons barked savagely as they passed.

They stopped to study a herd of a couple of dozen elephants who were breaking off branches from the trees and watching the approach of the car with much threatening spreading of ears and tossing of trunks. There were several huge bulls, also cows with calves. They were well off the trail, over humpy ground, and it was impossible to drive closer to them.

Hal, who wanted to photograph them, left the car, with the warden's permission, and walked towards them. The intelligent animals knew the difference between a camera and a gun and allowed him to come within a hundred feet. He took eight photographs. But when the world's biggest land animals found the fly-size human too annoying and seemed about ready to do something about it, Hal made a rather hasty retreat to the car.

Another half-mile and Crosby again brought the car to a halt.

'Now I'm going to show you something remarkable. You won't believe your eyes. Look over there.'

What the boys saw was a broken-down tree. An elephant stood beside it.

'What's remarkable about that?' asked Hal.

'Watch.'

The bark of the tree-trunk had already been torn off and the white wood was exposed. Presently the elephant raised his tusks and punched them deep into the wood. He exerted his great strength and, with a loud ripping sound, tore off a sheet of wood an inch or two thick and six feet long.

'What in the world is he going to do with that?'

For answer, the elephant coiled the end of his trunk round the board, lifted it from his tusks, and actually put it in his mouth.

Crunch, crunch – he chewed it up as if it were nothing but a potato chip. Within ten seconds the six-foot plank had disappeared into his great inside.

He tore off strip after strip, chewed, then swallowed. He evidently thought it a delicious breakfast.

'If he keeps that up,' Roger said, 'he'll soon be a wooden elephant.'

The boys had often seen elephants eating the leaves of a tree or even the twigs. But they had never before seen one eating the tree-trunk itself.

This was surely a freak of nature. 'I can't think of anything else in the world that eats trees,' Hal said.

'There's one,' Crosby replied. 'The termite. But it doesn't take a plank at a time.'

The elephant was so thoroughly enjoying his meal that he paid no attention to the car. He kept on filling himself with wood. Hal took photographs. People just wouldn't believe this unless they could see it in pictures.

'He was lucky to find a fallen tree.'

'Lucky nothing,' Crosby said. 'He probably pushed it over himself.'

'But that trunk is about five feet thick.'

'Well, the elephant is more than five feet thick, and his strength matches his size. We lose a lot of trees to the elephants. If they can't push a tree over they have another way of getting it down. They attack the standing tree on one side and keep cutting it until it falls. They are intelligent enough to step out of the way before it topples over. A young one who hadn't learned to do this was pinned under the tree when it fell. We found him three days ago still under the tree with his back broken. He died before we could get him out.'

The car climbed a steep trail to Poachers' Lookout. In front of a small pavilion a ranger stood with his eye glued to a telescope. He snapped to attention and saluted as the warden stepped out of the car.

'See anything?' asked Crosby.

'No, bwana,' said the ranger. 'Except some birds.'

Crosby looked through the telescope. He let Hal take his place, and then Roger. They could plainly make out some vultures circling over a spot at the edge of a wood. They flew round and round as they usually do over a dying or dead animal.

'Does it mean poachers?' Hal asked.

'I doubt it,' said Crosby. 'It's only about two miles from our lodge. Surely they wouldn't dare come that close. But we'll go down and take a look.'

They drove to the spot. A large black hulk lay at the edge of a grove of trees. There was no sign of any

poacher. As the men stepped out of the car a cloud of
vultures rose from the black body and climbed to join
the birds circling above.

'Dead rhino,' said Crosby, and led the way to the side
of the fallen animal.

The animal was more than dead. He was hollow.
There was a hole in his side as big as a barrel and his
insides were gone. Nothing was left but a big black cave
– and a terrible smell.

The boys stooped and looked into the cave. 'Poor
brute,' Hal said. 'Perhaps he fell sick and died and the
hyenas, jackals, and vultures chewed this hole in him.'

'Don't you think poachers might have done it?'

Hal stood up. 'Look. There are the bandas in full
view. The warden thinks the poachers wouldn't dare
come so close to the lodge.'

Crosby was studying the animal's head. 'That's what I
thought,' he said. 'But I was mistaken. Both horns are
gone. No animal would chew them off – they're not good

to eat. Poachers took them. And the animal didn't die a natural death.' He pointed to a ragged wound in the throat. 'A spear did that. Now you get some idea of how bold these fellows can be. But you haven't seen the worst yet. Jump into the car and I'll show you something that beats all this hollow.'

After only a few minutes' drive, the car stopped. 'This is the Tsavo River,' Crosby said.

The boys could see no river. There was nothing but a stretch of rough black rock.

'Have you ever walked on a river?' said the warden. 'Now's your chance.'

He led the way out on to the bare black area. He stamped on the rock. It gave out a hollow sound. Hal studied the rock.

'It looks like lava,' he said.

'It is lava. Some time or other it came down from Mount Kilimanjaro and covered the river. The river is still there – under your feet. Now let's walk downstream.'

As they walked they heard a rushing sound which steadily grew louder. They rounded a corner and then saw the river, gushing out in great volume and thunder from under the roof of lava. They could feel the roof tremble from the violence of the current. Released from its prison, the stream broadened here to form a large pool or small lake.

'This is called Mzima Springs. The water is usually as clear as glass.'

It was not clear now. It was reddish brown, and it stank.

'You've walked on top of the river,' the warden said. 'Now I'll take you under it.'

He brushed aside the bushes and revealed a slanting hole in the ground. They descended the steep slope in the half darkness and came out into an underwater room.

This must be the underwater observatory the warden had mentioned. Through windows they could look out into the heart of the river and up to its shimmering sunlit surface.

They eagerly pressed their noses against the glass. What they saw made them sick. Hippos – but they were not walking on the bottom grazing on the river weeds, they were dead and their carcasses lay in great heaps pressed down by more carcasses on top. Some, inflated by gases, had floated to the surface. Blood still trickled from the deadly wounds made by the poachers. Tails had been cut off, strips of hide had been removed, canine teeth of solid ivory, more valuable for some purposes than elephants' tusks, had been torn out, in many cases the entire head had been chopped off.

A few baby hippos, still alive, but nearly dead from starvation, prodded their senseless mothers who could no longer feed them.

The babies themselves were food for the crocodiles which glided after them, their great jaws wide open. These tender young bodies made a delicious breakfast for the great reptiles. The crocs churned the water with their powerful tails and even fought among themselves for the choicest bits. Hundreds of fish gobbled up fragments of hippo flesh.

The boys were sober as they climbed out of the observatory. They had been told that such things were happening – but they had to see it to believe it. They had been eager before to help stop the killing of animals by poachers. Now they were determined.

They returned to the lodge at nine and had breakfast. They had seen so much – it hardly seemed possible that they had been out only three hours. Now they must impatiently wait another three hours before their men would arrive and they could make their first expedition against the killers.

7

Blackbeard appears

At midday the fourteen lorries, trucks, jeeps, and Land-Rovers of Hal's safari rolled in.

Hal's thirty black safari men, with smiling faces behind a red film of road dust, climbed down. They showed plainly their affection for their young masters and the boys were equally pleased to see them – these fine, stalwart fellows who had been their partners in so many adventures, capturing live animals of every sort for the world's zoos and circuses.

The tents of the safari team were erected behind the row of bandas. The kitchen boys of the lodge set up a long table in the open air and loaded it with food.

The men ate hungrily but hastily because they were eager to get on with the job that they had come to do.

Warden Crosby addressed them. He told them of the poachers' camp that he and the boys had seen from the aeroplane seven miles to the west. He told them of the terrible slaughter of animals. He stirred them until they could hardly wait to get at the poachers.

There were cries of 'Let's go,' 'Break out the guns,' 'We'll murder them.'

Crosby held up his hand to quieten the men. 'I'm sorry,' he said, 'but that's the one thing you cannot do. You can't kill them. You will take no guns with you.'

'But they will have poisoned arrows, and spears,' objected big Joro, chief tracker. 'They will try to kill us.'

'Exactly,' agreed Crosby. 'And that's going to make your job dangerous and difficult. You see, there's a law against killing poachers. They have to be arrested and taken to court. They are tried and the judge fines them or puts them in prison. I know it doesn't seem fair – they will be well armed and you will not. You must not kill them – you must take them alive. You have had experience in taking animals alive. All right, these are animals – and you must capture them alive just as you would any other savage beast.'

The men were not smiling now. This was going to be worse than they had thought.

Hal spoke. 'Men,' he said, 'let's get one thing clear. This is not a part of your regular job. You were not hired for this. If you don't want to do it, you don't have to. Anyone who doesn't wish to take part has a perfect right to stay here in camp.'

When the cars started off a few minutes later not one man stayed behind. Hal was very proud of his crew.

In addition to his men there were five of Crosby's rangers. The other five were absent, looking for poachers in sections of the park more than a hundred miles away.

But there was one poacher-hunter perhaps as good as all of the five missing men. This one was not a man, but a dog – Zulu, the big Alsatian belonging to the safari man Mali.

Zulu had something that no other member of the party had – savage teeth. There was a law against guns. But there was no law against teeth. Zulu didn't know what this was all about, but he knew it was something great, and he barked excitedly.

Zulu's teeth would not be enough to win the battle. Crosby and the boys, sharing the same Land-Rover, discussed the problem as the cars bounced their way westward over the rough trail.

'There is a chance,' said Crosby, 'that they will take fright and run away when they see these fourteen iron monsters roaring in on them.'

'But you don't want them to run away,' Hal said. 'You want to arrest them.'

'Perhaps we can catch the ones who don't run fast enough. We may not be able to do all we want to do. We will just do what we can. I don't want to place your men in unnecessary danger.'

'Our men are used to danger,' Hal said. 'But do you really think the poachers will run?'

'It all depends. If they have no leader, they will run. If Blackbeard is with them, he will make them stand and fight.'

Hal had forgotten about Blackbeard, the man of mystery, whose real name was unknown.

'If we could nab him,' the warden said, 'that would probably end wholesale poaching in Tsavo.'

But how to do it? Deadly weapons were not allowed. What weapons could be used that were not deadly? Hal reviewed in his mind the contents of the supply van.

'How about sleep?' he said suddenly. 'Does the law say we can't put them to sleep?'

Crosby stared. 'Of course not. But how would you do that?'

'We do it with animals all the time. I don't know why it wouldn't work with poachers. If you'll stop the car and let me out I'll flag down the supply van and see if we have all the sleep we need.'

'I don't quite get you,' said the warden, stopping the car.

Hal hopped out. 'No time to explain now. See you later.'

In the supply van he busied himself filling several dozen darts with a thin white liquid. The darts looked harmless enough. They were only eight inches long and no larger round than your little finger. At one end of the dart was something like a hypodermic needle. At the other end was a tuft of feathers.

The van seemed to be twisting and turning. Hal put out his head. The cars had left the trail and were winding their way among termite hills ten to fifteen feet high built by the 'white ants'.

The fleet ground to a halt. Ahead was the thorn fence. The warden had stopped his car five hundred yards before reaching the fence and the other drivers had followed his example.

It would have been foolish to come close. Then the poachers could fire their arrows from behind the fence. Now it would be necessary for them to come out in front of it to attack.

Hal leaped out with a bucketful of darts. First he went to the warden.

'Will you help me distribute these?'

'What are they?'

'Darts – filled with dope.'

'Aco? But I told you – we're not allowed to kill ...'

'This won't kill anybody. It will just put him to sleep. It's Sernyl – muscular anaesthetic. Our men have used it in catching animals. They find Sernyl a hard word – so we've taught them just to call it Sleep. I've made enough for us to give each man three darts.'

The men had piled out of their cars and were looking for the enemy. There was not a poacher to be seen. Beyond the thorn fence among some trees were the poachers' grass huts, but there was no sign of life – except the life of suffering animals, struggling in snares in the gaps of the fence, raising pitiful cries of pain and terror.

The boys and the warden distributed the darts. But what good were darts if the poachers had fled?

The men lined up in front of the cars facing the fence. They were itching to get into action, disappointed at finding no enemy. A few of Hal's men became impatient and began to edge forward.

'Tell them to stop,' said the warden. 'All that ground is probably full of traps.'

At Hal's command, the men stepped back into line, grumbling.

'Look,' cried Roger suddenly, and pointed. Hal looked, and saw nothing. 'He's gone already,' said Roger. 'I saw him plain as day. He stuck his head out from behind the fence. A man with black whiskers. I'll bet it was Blackbeard.'

Perhaps the kid had just imagined it, Hal thought. The boy had Blackbeard on his mind.

The waiting grew tiresome, but Hal would not let his

men move. 'If there are any fellows hiding behind the fence,' he told the warden, 'it's just as well to let them think we're afraid to come on.'

Zulu, the big Alsatian, began to bark furiously. He started to run towards the barricade. His master, Mali, fearing the dog might be caught in a trap, called him back. The dog returned to the line but kept on barking.

Then a black head appeared in one of the gaps – then another and another.

'They're giving us the once-over,' Hal said. 'I hope we look harmless.'

Seeing no guns, the poachers grew bolder. They crept out through the gaps past the dead or dying animals. They were all well armed with spears and bows and arrows. Doubtless every arrow carried its smear of deadly poison. Black figures continued to appear until there were nearly fifty lined up in front of the thorn barrier.

The poachers stared as if they couldn't believe their eyes. These fools who had dared to invade their camp held no rifles, no revolvers, no bows, no spears, nothing but some little sticks. One poacher broke out into a laugh. It was taken up all down the line. It grew louder until it was a roar of merriment. Men doubled up with laughter and slapped their thighs and slapped each other and danced. A few arrows came flying, but they fell short.

The poachers began to pick their way forward, stepping carefully to avoid the traps concealed in the long grass.

'Be ready,' Hal called to his men, 'but don't fire till I

tell you.' Joro repeated the command in Swahili for those who knew little or no English.

Someone else was giving orders. He was not in the line of advancing poachers. He stood in one of the gaps of the thorn fence. He was not bare-chested and bare-legged like the men he commanded. He was dressed in a bush jacket and safari trousers and his whitish face was half concealed by the black beard.

'There he is,' Roger exclaimed. 'I told you I saw him. Blackbeard.'

'He's smart,' Hal said, 'to let his men do the fighting and save his own skin.'

Another sharp order from the man behind. The poachers at once slung their bows over their shoulders and took their spears from the back straps.

'Why do they change to spears?' Roger wondered.

The warden said, 'The arrow is for long-range fighting. At close range the spear is more deadly. They think we're unarmed – so they can come close. Watch out for those spears. They're poisoned too.'

The safari men had their eyes on Hal, waiting for his command to let go. Hal delayed until the poachers were within twenty feet.

'Ready!' he shouted, and each man raised his dart.

It really looked very silly. The poachers laughed again. Here they were, armed with poisoned spears eight feet long, and their enemy had nothing but toys no longer than pencils.

It was lucky, Hal thought, that the Sleep darts which his men had used in taking animals in Uganda and the Congo were unknown in this part of Kenya. The poachers were in for a big surprise.

But at the last moment Hal's plan was almost ruined.
The man with the black beard guessed the secret of those
innocent-looking toys. He shouted something in Swahili.
Joro said, 'He's telling them to fall back.'

It was too late. The poachers were too excited to obey
their master's voice. Victory was almost within their
grasp – why should they run now? The command did
make them hesitate a moment, and taking advantage
of that precious moment Hal shouted, 'Fire!'

The darts flew straight, guided by their tail feathers.
The needle tips plunged into black flesh. They did not go
in more than a quarter of an inch – they didn't need to.
The shock was enough to send the liquid flying into the
nerves beneath the skin, and these nerves telegraphed
the bad news all over the body.

The first result was terror. 'Aco!' yelled someone. The
cry was taken up by others. They all knew Aco, the
deadly arrow poison, and supposed at first that this was
what had hit them.

They hastily plucked out the darts. They saw that the
liquid dripping from the needles was white. They knew
that Aco was a brownish black. So this was not Aco.

This discovery gave them no comfort. Probably this
stuff was something new, even worse than Aco.

Whatever it was, it acted faster than arrow poison. It
went straight for the muscles and turned them into dish-
rags. Legs that were strong a moment ago became weak
and refused to hold up the body. The drug – plus fear –
paralysed the muscles.

Those who could run, ran – but soon fell in their
tracks. Some blundered blindly into traps that they had
set for the animals. Some who had not been hit at all

were so overcome by the general fright that they fell where they stood and prepared to die. A few of the braver spirits plunged forward and seriously injured three of the safari men with their sharp spears before they themselves were overcome by the numbing effect of Sleep.

Presently the place looked more like a bedroom than a battle-ground. Everywhere sleeping bodies sprawled in

the grass. Even those caught in the cruel traps did not cry out with pain, for they were unconscious.

Two who had run so well that they had almost reached the thorn fence were brought down by Zulu. Now they also were asleep.

'Into the Power-wagon,' Hal ordered. 'Into the cage.'

The Power-wagon was the truck generally used for carrying captured animals. In it was a huge elephant cage. The happy safari men and rangers dragged the sleeping poachers to the cage and thrust them in

Wire snares that had trapped some runaways were easily removed. It was not so easy to open the lion traps and elephant traps. These were like the bear traps some-times used in American forests, but larger and stronger. The teeth of the trap caught a man's ankle and dug in fiercely.

The warden, trying to free a sleeper from such a trap, called Hal and Roger.

'You remember I told you about two of my rangers who were caught in traps and eaten alive? You may have wondered why they couldn't free themselves. After all, a man has something the average animal doesn't have – two hands. Well, try to open that trap with your hands.'

Hal bent down, took hold of the two iron jaws and exerted all his strength to pull them apart. They did not budge.

'The spring is too strong,' he said.

'Right. It has to be strong to hold a lion or elephant. It can't be opened without a tool.'

Crosby saw Hal looking at the ten-foot chain that connected the trap with an iron spike driven into the ground.

'I know what you're thinking —' he said, 'that the ranger could have pulled up that spike; then he could hobble to his car with the trap still on his leg. Try to pull up the spike.'

Hal laid hold of the spike. He pulled until he was blue in the face. The spike did not move. It was driven into the base of a termite hill and the termites came out to see what was going on.

'You may as well give up,' Crosby said. 'That was

driven in with a sledge-hammer. About three feet deep into the hill. As you know, these termite hills are almost as hard as cement. Even an elephant couldn't pull that spike loose. Do you have a crowbar in your supply van? That would open the trap.'

Hal brought the heavy iron bar. He inserted it between the jaws, pried them open, and Crosby drew out the bleeding foot. Roger went for antiseptic and bandaging. Hal doctored the wounded ankle of the man who would gladly have killed him.

8

Blackbeard disappears

'AREN'T we forgetting something?' Roger said, looking back at the thorn fence. 'How about Whiskers?'

In the general excitement Blackbeard had been forgotten.

Hal leaped to his feet. 'Joro, Mali, come with me. Bring your dog. Toto, take over while we're gone.'

They dashed through the gap and looked around. Nobody.

He set off at a run for the gap where Blackbeard had last been seen. The others followed.

They dashed through the gap and looked around. Nobody.

'Look in every hut.' The huts were all empty.

Joro did not join in the search. When the others came back they found him squatting in the gap, studying the ground. He was Hal's best tracker.

The ground was covered with footprints, each ending in five dents made by the five toes, for the poachers went barefoot. There was one exception – a line of prints without toes.

'Made by boots,' Joro said. 'The boss – he wore boots. We catch him.'

He started out with great enthusiasm, following the boot-prints. He had not gone a dozen paces before he stopped, puzzled. There were no more boot-prints. It was as if the wearer of the boots had suddenly gone up in smoke. Could he have climbed into a tree?

Joro looked up. There was no branch low enough to be reached.

'He was smart,' Joro said. 'Took off his boots – so we no can track him.'

The ground was still covered with prints, but they all had toes. Who could tell which were the tracks of Blackbeard?

'The dog,' Roger suggested. 'Try the dog.'

Mali took his dog Zulu back to the gap. He bent the animal's head down so that his nose almost touched the boot-prints. Zulu sniffed. He followed the boot-prints to the point where they disappeared. The dog sniffed about aimlessly, making little whining noises.

Crosby shook his head. 'Your dog may be clever,' he said, 'but not that clever. Boots and bare feet don't smell alike.'

'You watch,' Mali said.

The dog went back and smelled the boot-prints – then the other tracks. Hal hoped against hope. It would all depend upon whether the boots were new or old. If they were new they would not have the smell of a man. But if they had been worn a long time in this hot climate they would have absorbed some of the perspiration and body-odour of the wearer. It would be faint, but a hunting dog's keen sense of smell might pick it up.

Zulu barked. He had found something. He went back again to smell the boot-print. Then with an excited yelp he started off on a trail of bare feet.

'He's got it,' cried Hal.

But the man who had made those tracks was not stupid. He had another trick to baffle his pursuers. A dead buffalo lay in a pool of its own blood. Blackbeard had walked straight through the blood. That should be enough to kill all man-scent. Where he had come out, who could say? – for the ground was covered with bloody footprints.

Crosby again shook his head, but Mali and the boys still had faith in Zulu's sharp nose.

Zulu took more time than before to make his selection. He finally picked out a trail but did not seem too sure about it.

Now the human tracker helped him out. Joro carefully studied and measured Blackbeard's prints leading into the blood and then the outgoing prints chosen by Zulu.

'Good,' he said. 'Dog, he got him. Foot, same wide, same long. Toes tight, boot.'

'What does he mean by that?' the warden asked.

'I think he means,' said Hal, 'that the toes are close together. That's a sign that the man generally wore boots. The boot squeezes the toes together. If a man always goes barefoot, his toes spread apart.'

Again they took up the trail. But again Blackbeard had a trick up his sleeve. The tracks led to the shore of the Tsavo River and entered the water.

Zulu howled his disappointment. He sniffed his way up along the bank, and then downstream, with no effect. Joro too was defeated. The hard river-bottom showed no prints. It was impossible to tell where the man had come out. He might have swum across the river, he might have waded upstream or downstream, and he would be careful to step out of the water into brush where he would leave no footprints.

'He's long gone by this time,' Hal said. 'Chances are, he went to where he had hidden his car and now he's well out of the park.'

Hal felt that his first attempt to help the warden had ended in failure. Crosby tried to cheer him up.

'Never mind. You caught the poachers. That's a good day's work.'

'But we let the boss slip through our fingers,' Hal said gloomily. 'He'll just start over again somewhere else with a new gang.'

9

The tiger-horse

FORTY-SEVEN poachers, sound asleep, were packed like sardines into the elephant cage.

They would stay asleep for about four hours – more than enough time to cover the hundred and thirty miles to Mombasa. They would wake up in the Mombasa jail.

Crosby wrote a note to the jail warden:

'Herewith, forty-seven arrested for poaching. Hold for trial.'

He gave the note to the driver. The Power-wagon, with its unconscious freight, took off.

The other cars remained, for there was still a job to be done – a painful job. The hundred or more animals caught in the mile-long trap-line and in the separate traps in the grass must be set free.

Black clouds of vultures flew up as the men approached the animals. Hyenas and jackals, that had been sinking their sharp teeth into creatures still alive, skulked away. They went just out of reach and stood waiting for a chance to rush in again to torture the screaming beasts.

The animals still able to fight struggled fiercely to escape from the wire nooses that had pulled tight on their necks. Every jerk made the wire sink more deeply into the throat. It cut like a knife into the flesh. Blood streamed down the animals' heaving flanks.

Roger and the warden tried to rescue a zebra from the snare that was choking it to death. It was dangerous to come near the animal because it was so mad with fear and pain that it lived up to its nickname of 'tiger-horse'.

A zebra is usually harmless. Although striped like a tiger, he is more of a horse than a tiger. But this zebra was more tiger than horse. His pain had turned him into a killer. He was ready to murder anything that came near. His strong teeth snapped together like a trap when the dog Zulu came too close. He could and did kick out with all four feet.

An iron-hard hoof caught the warden in the stomach and sat him down on the ground with a jolt. With the wind knocked out of him, he was too weak to move and

stayed where he was while hooves flew round him. If one
of them struck him in the face he might be killed. Roger
took hold of him by the shoulders of his bush jacket and
managed to pull him back out of the way.

Shakily, the warden got up. An experienced animal
man, he was ashamed that he had almost been laid low
by a striped horse.

'First time I've ever been saved by a boy,' he grinned.

Roger didn't tell him that it was the second time. The
warden already owed his life to the boy who had pulled
his helpless body off the control of the plunging aeroplane.

The warden pulled a wire-cutter from his hip pocket.

'We always carry these things when we go on rescue
missions,' he said.

'But how can you get close enough to use them?'

'It's not easy,' Crosby admitted. He staggered a little.
He was still dizzy. It wasn't just the kick of the tiger-
horse. He still felt the effects of his almost fatal experience of the day before. Perhaps there was still some Aco
in his veins.

Roger knew he must help. But he had no experience
with tiger-horses. He had tamed bucking broncos on his
father's farm. He could leap on to a horse's back without
benefit of saddle or stirrups. Then why be afraid now –
wasn't this just a horse? Not even as high as a horse. It
ought to be easy. He saw the dizzy warden pass his hand
over his forehead.

'Let me have the cutters,' Roger said.

'No, no,' the warden replied. 'I'll take care of this.'

'Let's both do it. You get in front of him and attract
his attention. I'll jump on his back and cut the noose.'

Crosby shook his head. 'Too risky.'

'For you perhaps,' said Roger. 'Not for me. I'll be on top – where he can't get me with either his feet or his teeth. You're the one who will have to look out.'

Crosby, half convinced, gave Roger the cutters. He went in front of the enraged beast, just out of reach of the huge yellow teeth that could snap off an arm and the sharp-edged forefeet that could split a man's skull right down to the Adam's apple. The frantic zebra lunged at him but was held back by the cruel noose.

Roger made a flying leap and landed neatly on the zebra's back. He leaned forward and snipped the noose. As it fell from the bleeding neck the animal plunged straight forward with a squeal of fury. The warden stepped out of the way. The zebra did not pursue him – he suddenly realized there was something on his back, something he had to get rid of.

He reared on his hind legs and tossed Roger upside down into the thorn barricade. The thorns went straight through the heavy bush jacket and safari trousers and tattooed the boy's skin. He struggled out to see the tiger-horse speeding away like a striped sail in a strong wind.

'Do you notice anything wrong with that zebra?' said the warden.

Roger studied the retreating figure. 'Well, there seems to be something missing. I know – he has no tail.'

'That's what made him so savage. Agony at both ends – neck cut, tail chopped off. That was all the poachers wanted – the tail. They lopped it off with a bush knife and left the animal there to suffer until he died. That tail is now a fly-whisk. Think of killing such a fine animal just so that some fool of a tourist can swat a fly. In the tourist shops in Nairobi you have probably seen trays full of fly-whisks made from the tails of zebras and gnus and other animals, and marked at some fancy price – and you've seen tourists buying them because they thought they would make amusing presents to take home to Boston or London or Paris. Many of those tourists are kind and gentle people, but they just don't think. If they could see the agony these beasts must suffer so that they can swat a fly, they wouldn't buy that fly-whisk.'

In the next gap were two snares, one set high to catch a large animal, one low to trap anything small.

In the lower one was a beautiful brown-eyed serval cat. In the upper snare struggled one of the handsomest creatures of Africa – the magnificent giraffe. Its throat was deeply cut by the wire noose. Plainly, it had not long to live.

Seven lions sat round it, licking their chops, waiting.

'I wish we could scare them away,' Roger said.

'That would hardly be fair,' said the warden. 'They have a right to their dinner. Nature made them meat eaters – like you and me. They are no more cruel than you and I are when we eat a beefsteak.'

'I know,' admitted Roger. 'It was the poachers who were cruel.'

Roger and the warden stood at a respectful distance, for it is not quite safe to interfere with seven hungry lions.

It has been said that a giraffe has no voice. That is not quite true – a low moaning sound came from the throat of the tortured animal. If it had been a buffalo or a rhino or an elephant there would have been a bellowing or grunting or squealing loud enough to be heard a mile away. But the near-silence of the tallest animal on earth and one of the most graceful was no sign that he did not feel pain. His feelings were revealed in the jerky twisting and wrenching of the body. Death would be a blessed relief.

'How long will he live?' Roger asked.

'Not long. An hour perhaps.'

'It's going to be a mighty bad hour for him. Can't we do something?'

'It's too late to save him.'

Roger put his hand in his pocket. 'I have one Sleep left. How about putting him out of his misery?'

'That's a wonderful idea,' said the warden. 'And it might work if you didn't have seven lions between you and the giraffe. Just how are you going to get round them?'

'I don't need to. I can throw the dart from here.'

'The hide is too tough. The dart wouldn't go in. You would have to jab it in by hand.'

Roger's eye followed the giraffe's neck up past the branch of an acacia tree.

'Why didn't I notice that before?' he exclaimed. 'That's the way to do it.'

Before the warden could reply Roger was halfway to the trunk of the tree. To get there he must pass within ten feet of the lions. Most of them were much too interested in the giraffe to pay any attention to him. But one, a huge male, evidently the leader of the pride, wheeled about to face him, laid back his ears, bared his teeth, crouched as if to spring, and let out a blast of thunder that tied Roger's nerves up in knots.

But he did not hesitate. He reached the tree and scrambled up. He could imagine the lion's claws sinking into his tingling back. Or the beast would catch one of his feet in its bone-crushing jaws.

He reached the lowest branch and looked down. The lion was standing on his hind feet with his front paws on the tree-trunk, and the look on the huge face was anything but pleasant.

Roger inched his way out on to the branch until he was close to the giraffe's head and neck. The great brown eyes with their remarkably long lashes looked at him appealingly.

He took the Sleep from his pocket and, with all his force, plunged the needle into the quivering neck.

He backed away from the thrashing head. He noticed a wire running down from the branch to the noose that held the little serval. Gently, he hauled the cat up out of the reach of the lions and planted its feet on the branch. He took out his cutters and snipped the noose.

Crosby watched anxiously. The excited cat might turn on the boy and scratch him badly. But the serval's only idea was escape. It ran along the branch to the trunk, then up into the safe treetop.

Roger was happy to see that the lion had gone back with the others, waiting for dinner. He slid down the trunk and sprinted to join the warden.

'That was a good job,' Crosby said. They watched as the drug took effect. The great eyes closed, the twisting and squirming stopped. The last hour of the great animal would be without pain.

Roger noticed that in this case too the tail was gone.
'To make a fly-whisk?' he asked.

'No. Some lady will wear the murder of that giraffe around her neck. They make necklaces out of giraffe tails.'

'And is that all the poachers wanted?'

'That, and just one other thing. Look at the backs of the hind legs. The sinews have been torn out.'

'What can they do with them?'

'Weave them to make a bowstring.'

So for a necklace and a bowstring this magnificent animal must die. It was just too pitiful.

In the next snare hung the body of one of Africa's loveliest creatures, the impala. Every visitor to Africa falls in love with the impala. It is a gazelle, the gayest of all the gazelles, so full of the joy of living that it cannot stay on the ground. It is a flier that does not need wings. It happily soars over bushes and small trees, touches the ground, then soars, and soars again. The vision of a hundred of these sleek, streamlined animals all in the air at the same time is a sight never to be forgotten.

But this impala would never sail again. The lovely creature was no longer lovely. A deadly wound had been cut in the neck by the wire snare. Parts of the body had been eaten away and maggots an inch long squirmed through the rotting flesh.

Roger could not bear to look at it. Heavy-hearted, he went on down the wall of death.

But the next animal was not dead – it was a Thomson's gazelle, usually called a Tommy. The Tommy is a friend of man. He never seems to learn that it is not safe to trust man.

Beside the trapped animal was a smaller animal that had not been trapped. It was a baby Tommy that had refused to leave its mother. The mother was kicking out savagely at some vultures that were tormenting the youngster. To the last she was thinking, not of herself, but of her fawn. The vultures flew away as Roger and Crosby approached. Crosby stooped beside the fawn.

'Too late,' he said. 'It's gone.'

Roger snipped the wire snare and the Tommy was free. But she did not run away. With her delicate little nose she nudged her baby to make him stand up, but she got no response. She herself tottered as if she might fall at any moment.

'Do you think we can patch her up?' said Roger.

'We'll take her to the hospital,' the warden said.

'Hospital?'

'Haven't you seen our animal hospital? We have a good many patients already but there may be room for a few more.'

Roger took the Tommy up in his arms. The slender little body weighed only some thirty pounds. Her blood soaked his bush jacket.

As he walked towards the trucks, she struggled fiercely, looking back at her fawn.

Crosby went back and took up what was left of the fawn. He carried it just ahead of Roger, and the mother Tommy was now satisfied and struggled no more. Her tired little head sank on Roger's shoulder. Her heart that had been beating violently against his chest slowed down and then stopped. Tommy had gone to the Tommy paradise, if there is one. At least the friend of man was beyond the reach of unfriendly man and his cruel traps.

Roger took a shovel from the truck and dug a shallow grave for the gallant little gazelle and her fawn. Then he set out to rejoin the warden who had already gone back to the trap-line.

10

Roger's cheetah

THE ground suddenly gave way beneath him.

He was falling. He clutched at bushes and grass but he kept on falling. It seemed he would never stop.

But Roger did stop, with a hard jolt, as he landed on the bottom some twenty feet below the surface.

He scolded himself. 'How stupid can you get?' He had been told to watch out for elephant pits. Now he had walked straight into one.

It was very dark. At first he could see nothing. Gradually he could make out the details of his prison.

It was large enough for the biggest of elephants. The walls were straight up and down. The roof was of brush, criss-crossed, and sprinkled with earth so that it would look solid enough to fool an elephant – or a careless boy.

He bumped against something hard. He examined it. It seemed to be a wooden stake driven firmly into the ground and standing five or six feet high. His fingers ran up the length of it and came to a sharp point at the end.

A sticky something came off on his fingers. He looked

at it, and then shivered. In the dim light he could see that the stuff was dark brown. It was Aco, the deadly poison the poachers used on the arrows.

He wiped his fingers on his trousers, hoping there were no scratches on his skin that would admit the poison to his system.

Now he could see that there were four such stakes in the centre of the pit. An elephant falling into the hole would be bound to land on them and they would mean his death. But before he died he would be in terrible pain. On so big a body the poison would not act quickly, so he might suffer for hours, even for days.

It was hard to believe that any men, even if they were poachers, could be so cruel. Most Africans were not brutal. He suspected that this pit of agony had been planned by the white man with the black beard.

Roger thought: Glad I'm not an elephant. I'd be on those stakes right now. Being considerably smaller than an elephant, he had fallen beside them, not on them.

A low snarl came from the darkest corner of the pit. Roger froze. It was bad enough to be in the pit alone – worse to be in it with the wrong kind of company. He thought of Daniel in the lions' den. But he didn't feel like a Daniel. He couldn't make friends with a lion that must already be furious at finding itself caught in such a trap.

Roger almost wished the lion had landed on a stake. But he repented of this thought immediately, for he wouldn't want his worst enemy to suffer that kind of death.

The beast stirred in its corner, still growling. Roger could see it a little more clearly. It was no lion. It was something much worse.

It was smaller than a lion, but more dangerous. He could see spots on its coat. It must be a leopard, and leopards were far more irritable than lions. Roger backed into the corner farthest removed from the angry beast.

Still the animal growled or snarled, but it didn't quite sound like a snarl or a growl. It reminded him of a cement mixer, or one of those chain saws the lumberjacks use in the Minnesota woods.

In fact it was very much like the purr of a house cat, only a hundred times as strong. As if puss were purring into a loud-speaker. Roger found it terrifying.

His uneasiness increased when he saw that the beast was coming towards him. Its big round golden eyes glowed as if they were lit from the inside. It didn't crouch like a leopard. It stood so high from the ground that it seemed to be walking on stilts. It had a bristling moustache and the hair on the back of its neck and shoulders stood up straight like that of a dog or cat that is angry or afraid. Two black lines running from the eyes to the corners of the mouth made it look more savage.

Roger rubbed his eyes. Was it really there? He wondered if his nerves were still upset by his experience with the leopard the night before.

Now a little more light fell on the beast. It was real, but the craziest leopard he had ever seen. It was so high from the ground, and behind it, switching to and fro, was a bushy tail a yard long ending in three black rings and a white tuft of hair.

Those spots – they weren't leopard's spots. Instead of uneven rings with light centres, these spots were round and solid black. Suddenly he remembered he had seen

pictures of this thing and had read about it. It was sometimes called a 'hunting leopard' – but it was no leopard.
It was a cheetah.

The cheetah is a dog-cat. It is like a cat and like a dog
and not quite like either. No dog, not even the Great
Dane, has such long legs. No dog can run so fast.

In fact, nothing on four legs can beat it. The cheetah
has been timed at seventy miles per hour. A Tommy
gazelle can go thirty-seven, a Grant gazelle thirty-five, a
zebra thirty, an ostrich twenty-nine, an elephant twenty-
five, and a rhino has to stretch himself to do twenty. A
cheetah quickly tires, but by that time he has caught
what he is after.

And that buzz saw – it was really a purr. It was a purr
to end all purrs. It made as much noise as a truck going
uphill. But whether the truck-like purr was friendly or
unfriendly, Roger still could not be sure.

The motor stopped and so did the cheetah. He cocked
his head to one side and his blazing eyes seemed to look
straight through the boy. Then an amazing sound came
from his throat. You might have expected to hear the
bark of a dog. But instead this was an ear-splitting
'miaow'! It was followed by a few little bird-like chirps.
To make them the cheetah puckered his lips as if about
to whistle.

The dog-cat-bird seemed to be asking a question.
Roger didn't know how to answer. Should he yell at the
top of his lungs to scare the beast away? Should he
growl like an angry lion? The cheetah was probably
afraid of elephants – should he scream like a charging
elephant?

He would have liked to run, but there was no place to

run to. He had shrunk back into a corner of the pit as far as he could go and he had no weapon to defend himself if the animal attacked – except the wire cutters. But whoever heard of fighting a savage beast with wire cutters? Still, they might do a good deal of damage. If the cheetah made a lunge at him, he might perhaps snip off that black nose, or plunge the cutters into an eye. The eye and the nose of any animal were particularly sensitive.

But what a pity it would be to spoil that handsome, savage face! Those wonderful golden eyes with sweeping eyelashes as long as the giraffe's, who could think of putting out for ever the light that shone in them?

Well then, there was only one thing left. Give the cheetah a polite answer to his question.

Roger tried to purr. It wasn't much of a success. It sounded more like a gargle. Perhaps he would do better with a chirp. He puckered his lips, but all he got was a whistle instead of a chirp. He said, 'Chirp, chirp,' but that was a failure too – it didn't sound a bit like the actual chirp of either a cheetah or a bird.

How about a miaow? It would have to be a super-miaow, as loud as the cheetah's. He put all his lung power into it. It was truly a noble performance, as miaows go, but it only made the cheetah cock his head to the other side and look puzzled as if trying very hard to understand this crazy two-legged creature.

Roger gave up the cheetah language and decided to try his own. He spoke in a low tone as he would to a pussycat.

'Here puss, here puss,' he said softly with a smile in his voice. 'Nice kitty, pretty kitty. Or if you prefer to be a dog, come Fido, here Fido.'

The tone of his voice did the trick. With one bound, the cheetah reached him, jumped up on him like a dog, punched his fore-paws into his chest and jammed him tightly back into the corner. The super-dog's head towered above his own and the open jaws with their great jagged teeth were within an inch of his forehead. His lungs were pushed in by the animal's weight. He gasped for breath.

His arms were free and he could have punched the beast or struggled to get away. Something told him that it was better to stand still and let Nature take its course. He had to admit to himself that he was terrified. The hair stood up on his neck as it had on the cheetah's. Prickles ran down his backbone.

Two gold lamps were peering through his head like X-rays. The beast lowered its head and opened its jaws wide. Roger had never looked anybody or anything in the teeth at such close range. It seemed to him those canines were as big as a hippo's. They appeared to be about to do to him what he had thought of doing to the cheetah – bite off his nose. The animal's hot breath flooded his face.

Then it came – the long tongue licking his cheeks, dog fashion. But unlike a dog's tongue, this one was quite evidently made of coarse sandpaper. It would take the skin off his face in no time.

'Now, Fido,' he said, trying to keep his trembling voice low and calm. 'Down, Fido, down.' He slowly raised his hand and scratched the animal's neck. Dogs liked that and so did cats. He wasn't so sure about birds.

The cheetah turned its head and seized his wrist in its jaws. Those terrible teeth could cut off his hand as easily as they could crush a rabbit. But he did not pull away. And the cheetah did not bite. The rascal was acting exactly like a dog that wants to play.

Roger put up his other hand and rubbed the beast behind the ears. The cheetah dropped the wrist and made a lightning change from dog into cat. It turned on its cement mixer. It rubbed its head against Roger's and its purr sent vibrations through his whole body.

Then it jumped down and went bounding about, chirping with pleasure. Its legs appeared to be made of steel springs. It could leap ten feet high with ease. Roger was anxious lest in one of its jumps it should come down on a poisoned stake. But every time it came down near a stake it skilfully twisted its body so as to avoid it. Then it would dash up to Roger and bunt him – and since it weighed more than he did, the bunt was nearly hard enough to knock him off his feet.

When he had had enough bunts he tried to give the playful animal something else to do. He pulled a root out of the earth wall and tossed it to the other end of the pit. The cheetah was after it in a flash. Roger thought he had never seen anything move so fast. The animal picked up the stick and raced back with it and laid it down at Roger's feet. Then it looked up at him, ears erect, eyes full of fun.

'That's a good dog,' Roger said. 'Nice pussy.'

He began to see why the animal was called a 'hunting leopard'. It could very easily be trained to hunt game like a hound. Perhaps it would even hunt poachers – like a bloodhound.

11

Mischief

ROGER heard voices.

'Where can that kid be?'

'When I left him he was digging a grave.'

'Where was that?'

'Near the supply van. But he's not there now.'

'Do you suppose he could have fallen into one of these pits?'

'Let's hope not. If he fell on the stakes he'd be dead by this time.'

Roger recognized the voices – Hal and the warden were looking for him.

He didn't want to be rescued. He had been having so much fun with the cheetah that he hadn't bothered to think how he was going to get out of this pit. He just wanted to go on playing with his new pet.

'Roger – are you there?' Hal was peering down through the brush. Roger heard him say to Crosby, 'I can't see a thing – it's so dark down there. But I thought I heard something move.'

He sounded so distressed that Roger took pity on him. He couldn't let his loving brother worry. He was just about to call back when he heard Hal say, 'It would be just like the stupid little runt to fall into one of these things.'

Just for that, thought Roger, I'll let you worry a little longer, you big clown. I don't need you. When I am good and ready I can get out of here all by myself.

He ran his hand over the wall of the pit, hunting for roots that would help him climb to the top. He found nothing that would bear his weight.

He heard Hal and the warden moving away. Sudden panic seized him. 'Hal!' he called.

'Did you hear anything?' he heard Hal say.

'Not a thing.'

'Just a moment.' Crunch, crunch – Hal's footsteps as he returned through the brush. Then his voice, 'Roger!'

'What can I do for you?' inquired Roger with mock politeness.

'You son of a gun! What a scare you gave us! Are you on a stake?'

The cheetah chose this moment to miaow. It sounded like a cry of pain.

'The poor kid is on a stake. We've got to do something fast. I'll get a rope.'

'I'm afraid it's too late,' Crosby said. 'That poison works fast.'

But Hal was already on the run to the supply van. He returned at once.

'I'm going to let this rope down to you. Do you have enough strength left to tie it round yourself?'

'I'll try,' said Roger as weakly as possible.

Down came the end of the rope. A sudden mischievous idea struck Roger and he almost laughed aloud. He put the rope round the cheetah's body just behind the front legs and tied it.

'All right,' he called.

The rope tightened. 'Wow, he's heavy,' Hal said.

'The stake is holding him. We'll have to pull harder to get him off it. Now, both together.'

Up went the cheetah. For him this was a new style travel and he didn't like it much. He snarled, and it was a real snarl this time, not a purr. It was an angry, growling, spitting cat whose head came up through the hole in the faces of the rescuers. They almost let him drop again, so great was their surprise. The cheetah scrambled out on to solid ground, showing an excellent set of savage teeth.

'A leopard!' cried Hal. Then he saw his mistake. 'No, a cheetah.'

Then he heard Roger's laugh, clear and strong. It was too hearty a laugh to come from anybody with a stake through his midriff.

Hal and the warden looked at each other grimly. 'You young devil!' Hal called. 'Wait till I get you out of there.'

That sounded like trouble. Roger was tempted to stay down until Hal cooled off. But how about the cheetah? Perhaps it would run away. He didn't want to lose it.

He needn't have been afraid of that. His new friend came back to the edge of the pit and looked down, whining. It danced about, showing every sign of pleasure when Roger was drawn up to the surface.

If Roger expected to be greeted like a prodigal son and have his big brother weep on one of his shoulders and the warden on the other, he was disappointed.

'Bend him over,' said Hal. 'Let me get a crack at him.'

The warden seized the young rascal behind the shoulders and bent him double over his knee. Hal spanked until his hand ached. He was stopped only by a sharp bite behind and a tearing sound as the cheetah laid open the seat of his trousers.

Then the three men sat down on the ground and laughed while the cheetah, seeing that things had changed for the better, pranced joyfully around them.

'He seems to have taken quite a liking to you,' said Crosby. 'It's lucky you got him before the poachers did. That gorgeous hide would be worth a couple of thousand dollars in New York. Cheetah coats are even more fashionable just now than coats of leopard skin.'

'Nobody's going to wear his coat,' said Roger, 'except himself. I'm going to keep him for hunting.'

'He'll make a wonderful hunter. A cheetah has a poor sense of smell, but marvellous eyesight – and he can go like the wind. He's easily trained – if he likes you. Never whip him. Never even scold him. He gets his feelings hurt very easily and then you can do nothing with him. Treat him well and he'll treat you well. He's nothing like a leopard – a leopard may become cross as it grows older, a cheetah doesn't. He's as faithful as a dog. You see, he's used to men – it's something that has grown into his nature because he has worked with men for more than four thousand years.'

'Four thousand years?'

'At least as long as that. On ancient Egyptian monuments you see pictures of men using cheetahs for hunting. Even today in Egypt cheetahs are used as watchdogs. Indian rajahs put a hood over the cheetah's eyes just as a falconer blindfolds a hawk. They take a hooded cheetah with them on the hunt. As long as the hood is on, the cheetah is quiet. When they come within sight of wild game, they take off the hood. The cheetah looks round, sees the prey, and goes after it like a bullet. When it catches up with the animal, it gives it one pat on the side. It looks like a very little touch, but it's enough to knock the animal flat. Then the cheetah picks it up, even if it is a good-sized antelope, and carries it back to the hunter. It still hangs on to its prey. I bet you can't guess how they make the cheetah drop it.'

'By saying "Drop it"?'

'It might not understand that order. But there's something it does understand. Gently pinch its nose. That shuts off its breathing and it will drop whatever is in its mouth.'

'Is it any good for catching poachers?'

'As good as any ranger. Better than a ranger – because it has better teeth. And gets over the ground three times as fast. We'll try it on the next poacher we see.'

12

Rescue

THE safari men set free all the animals that were still alive, and strong enough to stay alive.

The seriously injured were placed in the lorries to be taken to the hospital. Those nearly dead of starvation and thirst were given food and water at once.

The young, dying because their mothers had been killed, got special attention. A large cage was reserved for orphans. It was rapidly filled with as strange a crowd of babies as ever came together in one place – infant elephants, rhinos, wobbly little antelopes, lion cubs, and fluffy little monkeys.

The men went down into the elephant pits, rooted out the poisoned stakes, put them in a pile and burned them. One wall of each pit was broken down so that if an animal fell in, it could climb out.

The rescuers went from gap to gap of the mile-long thorn fence and collected every wire snare.

They broke up every devilish trap – the 'drop spear' set in a tree and triggered so that it would fall upon an animal passing below; the crossbow so arranged in a tree that just a touch of an animal's foot to the trigger-line in the grass would bring a poisoned arrow plunging down into its back; the cruel spiked wheel that would let an elephant's foot in but not out and poachers could then take their time removing his tusks and tail, then leave him to starve to death; the 'ant trap' set on the side of an ant hill so that the angry, two-inch-long ants would swarm over the trapped animal and devour it, after which the tusks could be more easily removed; the 'crippler' that when stepped on would fly up and break the animal's leg, making it impossible for him to escape the poachers – all the infernal devices that a diseased imagination could invent to inflict pain and death.

'Let's burn the fence,' Hal suggested, and the warden agreed.

The dry thorns leaped into flame and soon a bonfire a mile long was blazing.

Now the poachers' camp must be destroyed. First the contents of all the grass huts were brought out and put side by side.

'Never saw anything like it in my life,' Hal exclaimed as he looked at a collection of more than three hundred elephant feet that had been hollowed out to make wastepaper baskets.

In another pile were scores of leopard heads. Every one would have brought the poacher king several thousand dollars. The man from America or Europe who goes on a shooting safari in Africa hoping to get a leopard and mount its head on the wall at home to impress his friends, is apt to be out of luck. He is not likely to see a leopard, since it is a night animal. He gets tired of hunting for one. He finds it much simpler to go into a store in Nairobi and buy a head. Then he can take it home and mount it and claim that he shot it, and who will know the difference?

Here was a fortune in leopard heads. They would never get to the walls of would-be killers. Beside them was another fortune – a carpet of cheetah skins pegged out to dry. They would never adorn the backs of thoughtless women – sweet, kind women, quite unaware that they were the cause of the slaughter of beautiful animals.

Roger's cheetah, miaowing softly, nudged the skins with his nose as if urging them back to life.

'What in the world are those?' said Roger, staring at a large number of wooden bowls filled with curious curly hairs.

'Elephants' eyelashes,' said Crosby.

Roger looked at him suspiciously. The warden must be joking. 'You wouldn't kid me, warden?'

'Not a bit.'

'But who would want an elephant's eyelashes?'

'They're very popular all the way from here to Singapore. Superstitious men think that if they carry a little bag of these eyelashes they will have as many children as there are hairs in that bag. They're supposed to give you all sorts of magic powers. One pygmy chief I know traded fifty-two hundred pounds of ivory for the eyelashes of a single elephant. Some gangs of poachers make a business of killing elephants just to get their eyelashes. Dhows sail across the Red Sea to get eyelashes – they can be sold for high prices in Arabia because of the belief that a bag of eyelashes worn on a string round your neck is a sure protection against bullets.'

Near by was a pile of rhino horns that towered over Roger's head.

'What are they good for?'

'The Indians and Chinese pay big money for them. They grind them up into a powder. They mix the powder into their tea and drink it down.'

'Whatever for?'

'They think it makes them as strong as a rhino and as brave as a lion.'

'Does it have any such effect?'

'Only on the imagination. No physical effect. But the effect is very serious in Africa – it means that the rhino is disappearing. The rhino is one of the most interesting animals in Africa. Too bad if it has to go.'

'Look out,' cried Roger. 'You almost stepped on a big snake.'

It lay in the grass, a gleaming stretch of brown and yellow more than twenty feet long.

'A python,' Crosby said. 'He's dead. The poachers hadn't got round to skinning him yet. Of course python skin is worth a lot of money. Shoes can be made out of it, and belts, and handbags – all sorts of things. The flesh is good to eat – tender as chicken. But the best part is the backbone.'

He stopped and smiled, while Roger cudgelled his brain to think what anybody could possibly do with a python's backbone.

'African women make a necklace of it.'

'Just for decoration?'

'No. Another superstition. They think it's a cure for sore throat. Sometimes they make a belt of it. If you wear that round your tummy, you're supposed never to have indigestion.'

'How wild can you get?' was Roger's comment.

'Pretty wild,' admitted Crosby. 'Look at the stuff in these gourds. That's hippo fat – they use it as a pomade to slick down their hair. And that over there is lion fat. They rub it on for rheumatism.'

The warden's attention was arrested by a plot of fresh earth. Not a blade of grass grew in it.

'If I'm not mistaken,' he said, 'some digging has been going on here. Perhaps something is hidden underneath.'

He ordered men to bring shovels and remove the earth. Three feet down there was the gleam of ivory. The men threw out a beautiful elephant tusk. More tusks began to show up as they went deeper. Crosby counted as the tusks were tossed out on the growing pile. The total was five hundred and forty.

Crosby took out a notebook and did a little figuring.

'I'd guess that these tusks weigh about sixty pounds each. That comes to 32,400 pounds. Blackbeard has to pay his poachers about twenty pence a pound – he can sell the ivory for one pound eighty pence a pound. That would give him a profit of over £51,500.'

'I had no idea,' Hal said, 'that it was such a big business operation.'

'And murder on a big scale,' Crosby said. 'Five hundred and forty tusks – that means two hundred and seventy dead elephants. Just in one camp. And there are hundreds of such camps in East Africa. You think this trap-line a mile long is something. They are often five miles long, or ten, or fifteen. One discovered near Lake Victoria was seventy miles in length. In a single camp

we found the carcasses of 1,280 elephants.'

Hal knitted his brows. It was incredible. He could not
grasp such figures.

Crosby went on. 'Just in this one park we estimate
that we lose 150,000 animals a year to poachers. In East
Africa as a whole, poachers kill nearly a million animals
a year.' Crosby stopped and smiled. 'Perhaps I'm drown-
ing you in figures. But I'd like you to get an idea of how
serious this thing is.'

'Why don't the governments of these countries do
something about it?' said Hal.

'More easily said than done,' Crosby replied. 'They
can't afford it. It would take thousands upon thousands
of rangers.'

'But at this rate, soon the wild animals will all be
killed off.'

'Exactly. And that will be the end of the biggest zoo
on earth. Ninety per cent of the tourists who come to
East Africa come to see the animals. They bring in ten

million pounds a year. These countries will be poorer than ever if that revenue is cut off. Man is the most deadly of all animals. During the last two thousand years he has wiped out more than a hundred species. And the rest are going fast. At present two hundred and fifty kinds of animal are on the edge of extinction. Once they are gone, we can never get them back.'

13

Red dust

THE grass huts of the poachers were burned to the ground.

The tusks, tails, horns, hides, hippo teeth, elephants' feet, giraffes' sinews, leopard and lion heads, antlers of antelopes and gazelles, crocodile skins, lion fat, hippo fat, python backbones, feathers of egret, flamingo, ostrich, and crowned crane – all the trophies, including elephants' eyelashes, were loaded on the trucks. With them went all the snares and traps.

'What will you do with all this?' Hal asked. 'Sell it? It would bring a small fortune.'

'What it would bring would be blood money,' said Crosby. 'We don't want to make a profit out of murder. Anyhow, I think we'll accomplish more if we put these things in our museum where visitors from all over the world can see them. I don't think anybody can look at them without being shocked into doing everything within his power to stop this slaughter of innocent animals.'

Heavily loaded, the cars returned to the lodge. As Crosby and the boys entered the warden's banda they were greeted by smiling little Judge Sindar Singh.

'Well, my friend,' exclaimed Crosby. 'So good to see you again. Did you have a good trip to Nairobi?'

'Very good. On my way back to Mombasa now, but just called in to see how you got along with your raid.'

'It was a great success, thanks to these boys and their crew. Forty-seven poachers are on their way to your Mombasa jail right now. You'll probably have them in your court tomorrow morning.'

'Now isn't that just too wonderful,' purred the little judge. 'You can be sure of one thing – in my court they'll get what they deserve. We're going to stamp out this poaching – you and I. It's a disgrace and an outrage and must be stopped. I suppose you got their leader?'

'Blackbeard? No, I'm sorry, he escaped.'

'Now isn't that a pity – a great pity,' said the sympathetic little judge. 'How I'd like to get my hands on him! He wouldn't get out of my court without the stiffest sentence that the law allows. How in the world did he slip through your fingers?'

'He was too foxy for us, I'm afraid. He was wise enough to stay behind his men and while we were arresting them he got away. The dog followed his tracks but lost them in the river.'

The judge looked at Zulu. 'He's a fine dog. That Blackbeard must be pretty smart to outsmart such a fine dog.' He reached out his hand to pat Zulu. The dog sniffed at him, then backed away, growling.

'Well, I must be going,' said the judge brightly. 'What a fine cheetah! He seems to be making himself at home already. How do he and the dog get along?'

'We hardly know yet,' said Hal. 'So far, they've politely ignored each other.'

'We'll see you off,' said Crosby, and they all walked out with the judge to his car.

Hal noticed something strange about the car. There was no red dust on it.

He had been over the Nairobi road several times. It was a dirt road with murram stacks along the edge – piles of red earth used to surface the road. You could not travel this road without getting your car covered with red dust.

Murram was not used on the roads inside the park. There too a car would pick up dust, but it would be white. There was a film of white dust on the judge's car.

'How did you escape the red bath?' Hal asked.

The judge seemed a bit surprised by the question, but he responded quickly enough. He laughed a silky laugh.

'Yes, yes,' he said. 'You certainly get plastered on that road. So I stopped at the petrol station just before entering the park and had the car washed.' He smiled. 'Any more questions?'

'No,' said Hal, a little ashamed of having quizzed the good judge. But Singh did not appear to be offended.

He spoke to Crosby. 'Goodbye, Mark. Take care of yourself. I congratulate you on having these boys to help you. Perhaps they'll even be smart enough to catch Blackbeard. Who knows?'

And he was off.

Zulu and the cheetah were getting acquainted. They were not very polite about it. They drew back their lips, each trying to show what a fine set of teeth he had.

Zulu barked. The dog part of the cheetah growled. The cat part spat.

Each was acting exactly as Nature had taught him to act. The Alsatian is a born police dog. He takes no nonsense from either man or animal. The cheetah is a born hunter of other animals including wild dogs. And this one looked wild enough.

'Zulu, come here,' said Roger sharply. 'And what's-your-name – I'll call you Chee – behave yourself.'

Chee who had evidently been planning to make a meal of this dog changed his mind when he saw his young master patting Zulu. He came up on Roger's other side, nuzzling the boy's leg and miaowing softly. Roger patted him also.

The two animals were not quite ready to be friends. They suddenly made a lunge for each other between Roger's legs, tumbling him on to his back.

'Chee! Zu!' Roger jumped to his feet, caught Zulu by the collar and brought him face to face with Chee. Their muzzles were not an inch apart. He held them so, Zu by his collar, Chee by his silky mane. The dog in each of them whimpered. There was no barking this time, no spitting. These fine animals were not stupid. They got the message.

Roger let them go and each retired in a different direction to lie down and think it over.

'How are we going to feed Chee?' Roger asked. 'No telling how long he was in that pit. He must be hungry.'

'That's easy,' Hal said. 'Just tap a vein in your wrist and let him drink the blood.'

'You think you're pretty funny,' said Roger scornfully.

'No,' put in the warden, 'your brother is right. There's nothing the cheetah would rather have than blood. But it doesn't have to be yours.'

'We might let him go and hunt his own food.'

'If you do that, you'll probably lose him. If you want him to stick to you, you had better feed him.'

'But how?' Roger had a sudden idea. 'Those animals we brought to the hospital – did any of them die?'

'No, and we mean to see to it that none of them will die.'

'Then how...?'

'Jump in the car,' said Crosby. 'I'll take you where you can get plenty of blood. And nothing will have to die to give it to you. Bring Chee.'

Roger called Chee but the animal did not know his name. Roger went to him and tugged on his mane. Chee took this only as a friendly gesture, and purred.

Crosby laughed. 'I see you don't know how to lead a cheetah. Take him by the teeth.'

Roger stared. This time for sure the warden was joking.

'A cheetah has very long canine teeth,' explained Crosby. 'His incisors and molars are very short. You can slip your finger in behind a canine. The short teeth will close on your finger but, if he likes you, he won't close them tightly enough to hurt. Of course you're taking a chance – he may decide he doesn't like you after all. If it works, you can lead him anywhere.'

'And if it doesn't work,' said Hal comfortingly, 'all you lose is a few fingers.'

Roger gave Hal a savage look. His big brother was trying to scare him. He didn't need to try hard – the boy was already scared. The nerves crawled around in his back like worms as he very cautiously pressed Chee's lips apart, then slowly put his finger in between the short teeth and round the canine. This was the craziest thing he had ever heard of. Surely Chee would bite.

Chee did bite. But it was not a hard bite, only a squeeze. For a full minute, Roger kept his finger in place without making any further move. With his other hand he scratched Chee behind the ears.

Then he began to pull, very gently. Chee unwound himself and got up. Roger waited a moment – then began to move towards the Land-Rover. Chee tightened his grip ever so slightly and followed.

Getting into the car without jerking his hand or exciting his pet was an experience that Roger would not soon forget. Inch by inch, with frequent pauses, he sidled up into the seat, still keeping his fingers in the animal's mouth. In fact he could hardly have let go if he wanted to, the pressure on his fingers was so firm.

Luckily Chee had already had one ride in the car. No harm had come to him, so now he did not seem to be unduly nervous. He stood up on his hind legs with forepaws on the car floor. A light spring, and he was in the car between Roger's knees. His jaws relaxed and Roger withdrew his hand. The fingers were dented but not bruised. The powerful jaws that could crush a baboon's head as easily as a hammer can crack a walnut had been controlled by the animal's natural gentleness and intelligence.

14

A cheetah's dinner

SINCE the lodge was close to the park edge it was only a matter of minutes before the car left the park and came to a stop beside a thorn fence.

This was no trap-line. It was a wall of thorns round a small village.

'To keep wild animals out?' inquired Roger.

'No,' said Crosby, 'to keep cattle in. These Masai are cattle-men. You might call them the cowboys of Africa. Come in and meet them.'

He led Roger and his cheetah through a thorn gate into the village. Roger had seen some strange villages, but never anything like this. The huts were more like ant-hills than houses. The only difference was that the homes of the ants were usually bigger and higher. The roofs of these were on a level with Roger's chin.

'Look as if they were made of mud,' Roger said.

'That's about it. They make a framework of twigs, then plaster it over with clay and cow-dung.'

'But the doorways are only three feet high. Are these people pygmies?'

'Far from it. Watch.'

A man came out of the nearest hut. To get through the low door he had to bend almost double. When he straightened up he was more than six feet tall – almost as tall as the Watussi Roger had seen in the Mountains of the Moon.

'Why such low doors for such tall people?'

'They have a good reason for it,' said Crosby. 'If some enemy tries to enter your home, he has to bend far down to get in. He can't defend himself in that position. He can be knocked on the head or jabbed with a spear before he can get all the way through the door.'

Other men came stooping out of the mud huts. They smiled when they saw Crosby, who was evidently well known to them and well liked.

Each man wore a cowhide cape over his shoulders and nothing else. His hair was plastered with red clay and worn in a short braid over the forehead and a long braid behind. His ears had been pierced and stretched so that they hung almost down to his shoulders and the hole that had been bored in the ear-lobe in childhood had been pulled larger and larger so that in a man of middle age it was big enough to carry a good-sized package. Which was lucky, since a man's cape had no pockets.

When any man smiled Roger could see that he had two teeth lacking in the lower jaw. He asked Crosby about it.

'These people sometimes get lockjaw. Then the teeth lock together so that they can't eat or drink. They knock out two teeth so that if they contract this disease they can still get food and drink into the mouth.'

'But lockjaw can be cured. Don't they call a doctor?'

'They don't believe in doctors. In fact they don't believe much in anything that is modern. They stick to their own way of doing things.'

A fine-looking Masai approached Roger with a smile and spat in his face. Roger wiped his face. He looked so astonished that Crosby had to laugh.

The Masai waited as if expecting something.

'Spit back,' said Crosby.

Roger could not believe his ears.

'Spitting in your face is a sign of friendship,' the warden told him. 'Don't keep him waiting or he'll be offended. Spit back.'

Roger summoned up all the saliva he could gather and spat back. The big Masai grinned from ear to ear.

Women and children began to emerge from the huts. They were too timid to come near. The little brown bodies of the children were bare. The women were dressed in metal – but their armour was not like that of the knights of old. Their arms were buried in metal bracelets, they wore necklaces of metal beads, huge metal earrings several inches wide hung from their ears, metal ornaments circled their waists, and their legs were completely buried from ankle to knee under wire spirals. The wire was the only thing that looked modern.

'Where do they buy the wire?'

'They don't buy it. They just steal it from the nearest telephone line.'

Roger could not help noticing that these primitive people were not dirty. 'For people who live in mud huts they keep themselves remarkably clean. They must bathe twice a day.'

'Hardly,' Crosby said. 'They get only two baths in a

life-time – one at birth and the other when they become adults.'

'Then how do they keep clean?'

'Sand. Have you ever tried a sand bath? It will take the skin off you if you're not used to it. These people are used to it and it just takes off the dirt.'

Crosby spoke to the Masai in their own language. He pointed at the cheetah and at one of the cattle that strayed among the huts. The men nodded vigorously, and one of them ran into a hut and came out with a bow and arrow.

'We're going to get some blood for your cheetah,' Crosby said. 'But without killing anything. We've come to the right place. The Masai are like the cheetah – they live on blood. Blood and milk. Perhaps it's the strangest diet of any people in the world – although some of the reducing diets in your country are just about as strange.'

'You don't mean the Masai live on nothing but blood and milk? No meat, vegetables, fruit?'

'A few of the modern ones will take a little meat, perhaps on a holiday. Most of the people won't touch it. And never a vegetable of any sort, or a soup, or a salad, or a bun or biscuit or bread of any kind, or pudding or cake. No cheese, no butter, no eggs, no jam or jelly, nothing sweet, no fruit of any description.'

'Just blood and milk,' marvelled Roger. 'How can they live on that? You'd think they'd dry up and blow away. But they look pretty strong.'

'They are strong. And brave. A Masai will wrestle with a lion or a leopard. A young Masai must kill a full-grown lion with nothing but a spear before he can claim to be a man.'

Roger looked at the cows. 'That's where they get the milk. But how about the blood?'

'Come. We'll show you.'

The man with the bow and arrow selected a cow. He came to within six feet of it, dropped on one knee, and aimed at the animal's throat.

So, thought Roger, that was all guff – about not killing anything. He's certainly going to kill that cow.

The cow did not seem to be alarmed. She peacefully chewed her cud. The bowman fired his arrow and it struck home. The cow went on peacefully chewing her cud as if nothing had happened.

Roger noticed that the arrow had penetrated only a fraction of an inch. A shoulder behind the tip had prevented it from entering farther. The point had evidently been so sharp that the animal had not felt it.

The bowman pulled out the arrow and blood poured from the jugular vein. Another Masai caught the blood in a large gourd. The cow stood as patiently as if she were merely being milked.

When the gourd was full a sort of dirty-looking paste was applied to the small hole.

'A mixture of ashes and herbs,' Crosby said. 'You see how that stops the flow. It will also prevent infection.'

The Masai spoke to Crosby and kept glancing at Roger. The warden nodded, and one of the men dived into a hut and brought out a small gourd. From the large gourd they poured about half a cupful of blood into the small container. Then one crouched beside the cow's udders and filled the small gourd with milk. With his finger he stirred the two liquids together – then offered the gourd to Roger. Roger looked helplessly at the warden.

'Drink it,' Crosby advised. 'They're trying to be nice to you. Don't let them down. You'll hurt their feelings.'

'How about my feelings?' grumbled Roger.

'Never mind your feelings, young man,' said Crosby rather sharply. 'In Africa you show respect for the Africans. If you don't we have unpleasant incidents like the Mau Mau massacres when even our wives have to carry revolvers and no white man's life is safe.'

'I get you,' Roger said meekly and raised the gourd to his lips. He drank down the contents without stopping, trying not to taste the stuff. But when he got it down he realized that it had not been unpleasant after all.

The effect upon the Masai was magical. They chattered and grinned and patted his arm. Now they really accepted him as a friend.

It was Chee's turn – but for him, no milk thank you. He eagerly lapped up the fresh blood. In the meantime the Masai insisted upon tapping another cow so that Chee would dine well tomorrow.

On the way back to the lodge Roger had some questions to ask.

'Do the Masai raise cattle just to get their blood?'

'Oh no, they must have cattle to buy wives. A man must pay three or four cows to the girl's parents. The more cattle he has the more wives he can buy. A Masai's wealth is reckoned in cattle, not in money. He may not have one solitary coin, but if he has a hundred cattle he is a rich man.'

'Because he can sell them and make a lot of money?'

'No. He refuses to sell them. If he sold them, he wouldn't have them. He would have nothing but money, and he doesn't care a hang about money. All he cares about is cattle. That's what makes him such a problem.'

'How so?'

'There are a hundred thousand Masai and they own about a million cattle. These cattle destroy thousands of square miles of land. They eat not only the grass above ground but the roots as well, so grassland becomes desert. Wild animals do not eat the roots, and grassland remains grassland. The Masai don't need so many cattle, but we do need plenty of food for wild animals if we hope to keep on bringing tourists here to see the greatest zoo on earth.'

They stopped at the river to let Chee drink. Chee walked to the water's edge, looked upstream and down stream and across. He hissed loudly, then drank.

'A wise cat,' said Crosby. 'He hisses to scare the crocs away. A lion or a leopard or an antelope would probably just stick his nose into the water and drink. Then a croc might grab him by the nose and pull him in. A cheetah is too smart to take that risk.'

Chee bounced back into the car without being led. He wasn't satisfied to stay on the floor. He tried to climb up on the seat beside Roger. Roger slid over to the centre to give him room and Chee sat up beside the open window.

The animal chose to thrust out his head just as the car passed close to a group of tourists. A woman screamed, 'Look! They've got a tiger in that car.'

The warden grinned and stepped on the accelerator.

'The old story,' he said. 'Everybody knows or thinks he knows about the tiger or the leopard or perhaps the jaguar. But not one in a hundred has ever seen the cheetah – the friendliest of all the big cats.'

Chee was sometimes almost too friendly. At night he insisted upon sharing Roger's bed. And since he was a good seven feet from nose-tip to tail-tip and his long legs reached three feet across the bed there was not much room left for the boy. To make matters more difficult, he purred like a grist mill in Roger's ear. But it would take more than that to keep a healthy young teenager awake after such a big day.

15

The trial

'SOMETHING on your mind, Hal?'

Crosby had noticed that Hal was merely toying with his breakfast, letting his coffee grow cold. He had not joined in the conversation with the warden and Roger – and Chee, who was as usual purring so loudly that the others had to raise their voices to drown him. Hal's thoughts seemed far away.

He looked up and smiled. 'You just caught me dreaming.'

'Anything I can help you about?'

Hal hesitated. 'Well – yes. It's about – your friend, Judge Singh. You think a lot of him, don't you?'

'I suppose I do,' admitted Crosby. 'He goes out of his way to be friendly and helpful. He's done all sorts of things for me. Even saved my life the day before yesterday – you saw him do that.'

'It wasn't . . .' exploded Roger, then stopped as he saw a warning in Hal's eyes. He itched to say that it had been Hal who had saved the warden, not Singh. Singh had almost killed him.

'And the judge is my best ally against the poachers,'

Crosby went on. 'We could really do nothing without him. We can catch some of them but we can't punish them. They are punished in his court – he fines them or sends them to prison. The law allows very heavy sentences for the crime of poaching.'

'Does he give them all the law allows?'

'Yes, he says that he does.'

'Have you been down to his court?'

'Oh no. I'm too busy here. I do my job and let him do his.'

Hal went back to his eggs and bacon. He ate in silence for a few minutes. Then he said, 'An interesting man, the judge. I'd like to see him at work. How about our hopping down there this morning to take a look at the trial?'

'I can't go,' said Crosby. 'But there's no reason why you shouldn't. Only trouble is – it's a 250-mile trip to Mombasa and back and the road is pretty bad. But then – what am I thinking of? You're a pilot. You proved that when I went to sleep on the stick. Take the Stork. Wait a minute.'

He went to his desk and brought out a map.

'Now – here we are – and here's Mombasa. As you know, it's on an island connected with the mainland by causeways. Here's the landing field.' He made a cross with his pencil. 'You'll get a taxi there and go to the court-house – which is here.' He made another cross.

On the airstrip, Crosby superintended the fuelling of the Stork, filling both wing tanks, also an emergency tank in the back of the plane. He pointed out the little hand pump that would transfer this petrol, if needed, to the wing tanks.

He translated the German instructions on the instrument board and explained some of the mechanical mysteries that had baffled Hal.

'Get full steam up before you take off,' he said. 'Otherwise you'll never clear those trees at the end of the strip.'

Hal climbed aboard. Roger was about to follow but his brother stopped him.

'Stay out of it, kid. I want a little practice first.'

'Can't you practise with me aboard?'

'Just let me take it up – and come down again. Then I'll pick you up.'

Roger began to object but Crosby cut in.

'Your brother's right. It's a touchy take-off.' Roger looked disappointed and a little angry. If Hal could take this risk, why couldn't he? The warden smiled. 'I can't afford to lose you both, you know.'

'I'll be back in five minutes,' Hal said. 'Sooner than that if I forget which button to push.'

He looked at the wind-sock. It didn't give him much encouragement. It ought to be blowing up or down the strip. It was blowing across. On a narrow strip, walled in by trees, this could mean trouble.

He let down the Perspex hood, thus completely enclosing himself in the transparent bubble. Looks like a dummy in a store window, thought Roger crossly.

Hal started the ignition. He tested the booster pump and waited for the oil temperature to rise.

He taxied to the end of the strip and turned about. Down went the throttle. The plane moved, but too slowly. Hal gritted his teeth as if that would help the engine. He wished the strip were asphalt instead of grass. The plane stumbled on, gathering speed.

Now it was floating on the blades of grass. Now it was in the air.

Hal set the flaps at fifteen degrees for extra lift. The trees at the end of the strip were coming towards him at an alarming rate.

He was worried too about the cross-wind that kept pushing him to the right. This was a small plane, as planes go, but still its thirty-nine-foot wing span seemed too much in this narrow trap.

The end of the right wing was already tickling the leaves of the trees. A small branch, no thicker than a finger, would be enough to send the whole contraption crashing to the ground.

He cleared the trees by inches. Now he had time to think of the things he might have done – give it a bit more flap, trim back the elevator a little farther, keep the nose closer into the wind – he would remember and do better next time.

He circled until his nerves settled down, then straightened out towards the strip and prepared to land.

Full flaps, speed down for the approach, ruddering to fishtail off the height – he skimmed the treetops, sank like a falling leaf and touched the grass. Now he knew where the brakes were, and used them.

The plane lumbered over the none-too-smooth ground and came to a halt. Hal opened his bubble.

'Good enough,' said the warden heartily. Even Roger, still a bit sulky, had to admit it wasn't bad. He climbed into the co-pilot's seat.

This time the plane seemed to know its master. It rose as a plane should, levelled off at six thousand feet, and followed the Tsavo River eastwards to the railway station at Tsavo.

Here Hal swung to the right. Below him was the red road to Mombasa and beside it the railway.

This had been the scene of very tragic events. Years ago when the railway was being built, newspapers all over the world were running horror stories about the 'man-eaters of Tsavo', lions that had developed a taste for human flesh and were killing and eating railway workers by the score in spite of all efforts to track them down.

On the left now was the gleaming ribbon of the Galana River on its way to the Indian Ocean. Northward stretched the wilderness of Tsavo Park for a hundred miles.

The foaming waters of Lugard's Falls flashed white in the morning sun. Around the pool at the base of the falls elephants, rhinos, and giraffes were stooping to drink. Animals were clustered around a lake and several water holes. Herds of buffalo, zebra, and wildebeest were mowing the grass in the open meadows. The day-loving lions were out looking for breakfast, but the night-loving leopards had retired into the darkness of the woods.

A thin spiral of smoke rose from the trees.

'A poacher's camp,' Hal guessed.

'And there's a trap-line,' exclaimed Roger. 'Oh boy – what a long one. It must be a good five miles.'

Hal did some mental arithmetic. 'That would come to around twenty-six thousand feet. And if there's a trap every fifty feet that would come to something more than five hundred traps. Suppose only half of them caught animals.'

'Suppose nothing of the kind,' said Roger. 'Yesterday there was an animal in every single trap.'

'All right. And the poachers clear the traps once a week. Five hundred dead animals a week – more than two thousand a month. I can't believe it. Must be something wrong with my figures.'

'What does it matter?' Roger said. 'Even a hundred a month would be a hundred too many. And don't forget, this is just one trap-line. And the warden says there are others two or three times as long. And hundreds of trap-lines all over East Africa.'

It was easy navigation. All you had to do was to follow the road and railway. Actually the road could not be seen because it was concealed beneath a continuous cloud of red dust stirred up by traffic. The ribbon of red wound down to Mombasa, already visible on its coral island set like a jewel in the blue of the Indian Ocean.

The plane landed lightly on the broad airfield eight miles from town and the boys took a taxi across the causeway and through the busy streets of the island city to the court-house.

Hal peered in through the crack between the double doors.

At the far end of the room behind a desk on a high platform sat Judge Sindar Singh. He did not look so little now. His black robe gave him importance and dignity. Before him stood the poachers, all of them. The rest of the room was full of spectators, also standing. There was no jury, no prosecutor, no defender. Judge Singh was the sole authority. This was not a criminal court – strangely enough, the murder of helpless animals was not considered a criminal offence.

'I'd rather the judge didn't see us,' Hal whispered. 'Let's duck our heads down and sneak in as quietly as we can.'

They slipped through the door and stood behind the crowd.

An interpreter was questioning one of the prisoners in his native dialect, then passing on the answers to the judge in English.

'He says,' explained the interpreter, 'that he is a poor man. He has eight children. And four more on the way.'

'Four on the way?'

'Yes. He has four wives.'

The judge looked severe. 'Does this man realize that I could send him to prison for ten years for poaching?'

'Yes, he knows that.'

'But this court has mercy upon the poor and unfortunate. I will not punish this man. Any man with four wives is being punished enough already.'

The crowd laughed. What a jolly little judge this was!

'Case dismissed,' said Judge Singh.

But not everyone was amused. An intelligent young African standing next to Hal whispered angrily, 'He's being too easy on them. You can never stop poaching that way.'

Hal nodded. He thought of all the trouble and danger he and his men had gone through to catch these fellows. And now they were being let off with little or no punishment. Of course they would go right back to poaching.

The judge was questioning the next man. 'Don't you know it is wrong to kill animals?'

'No. My tribe has always killed animals. It is our

custom. Our fathers killed, their fathers killed, for ever it has been so.'

The judge meditated. 'How can we ask this man to go against the custom of his tribe? Case dismissed.'

The next man had a different excuse. 'I am a kind man. I do not like to kill. But the black-bearded one, he makes us kill.'

The judge nodded solemnly. 'You do not do it of your own free will?'

'Never.'

'This black-bearded one is a devil. You are afraid of him, are you not?'

'We all fear him.'

'That is good. I mean,' stumbled Judge Singh, 'it is good that you do not do this willingly. How can I punish you if you do only what you are forced to do? Case dismissed.'

The next prisoner when asked why he was guilty of poaching explained that he had a flock of goats, and wild animals were killing and eating his goats – so he must kill the wild animals.

'What wild animals do you kill?'

'Mostly rhinos, giraffes, elephants, hippos, zebras, antelopes.'

'You cannot be blamed for defending your flock against these wild beasts,' declared Judge Singh. 'Case dismissed.'

The African at Hal's elbow boiled over. 'Every one of those animals eats grass and nothing else. Not one of them ever ate a goat. This whole thing is a farce and a fraud.'

He turned and left the room.

16

Old Harbour

THE boys also had had about enough. But they stuck it out – they listened to the lame excuses of all forty-seven prisoners. The judge, realizing that it would look too ridiculous for him to say 'Case dismissed' every time, imposed a few light sentences.

One man was sent to prison, not for ten years, but for three days. He grinned when he heard his sentence. He could rest in prison and would get better food than he would have at home.

Another man who had a small farm on which he raised melons was fined one melon.

Another who raised chickens was ordered to pay a penalty of two eggs.

Most went scot free.

Hal and Roger left the court-room without having been seen by the judge. They were gloomy, angry, and bewildered.

'We break our necks to catch poachers,' grumbled Roger, 'and he lets them off.'

'And that means we've really done more harm than good,' said Hal. 'Now these fellows know that they can poach all they like and if they're caught they'll just have a nice trip to town at somebody else's expense.'

'What's the matter with that crazy judge?' wondered Roger. 'He had so many big things to say about what he would do to the poachers. All that big talk about protecting the wild animals. He certainly has the warden buffaloed. You know what I think? I think he's in league with Blackbeard. I'll bet they're in this thing fifty-fifty. They're splitting the profits right down the middle.'

Hal shook his head. 'He seems like such a kind sweet little man. And Blackbeard is such a devil. How could they possibly have anything to do with each other? Until we know more about it we'll have to give the judge the benefit of the doubt. Perhaps he really thought he could win those poachers over by kindness.'

'Kindness my hat!' exclaimed Roger. 'Is it kind to the animals to let a gang of killers loose on them?'

They walked slowly down the street. Roger, irritated because his brother refused to think ill of the judge, stopped short.

'Look here. We'll do some detective work. You say he's an angel and he's just trying to be good to the Africans. I say he's a devil and he's working with Blackbeard. We'll just see who's right.'

Hal smiled and said nothing. He had a suspicion that they were both wrong. There must be some other explanation for the judge's strange conduct. He really didn't think that the judge was an angel. In fact he might be even more of a devil than Roger imagined. Time would tell.

In their aimless wandering they had left the main streets with their fine modern buildings and found themselves in the maze of narrow alleys of the old Arab town.

Open doorways led into dark, mysterious shops. From some came the odour of fruits and vegetables, from others the smell of fresh meat.

One had the peculiar scent of wire and iron and something prompted Hal to step inside.

He saw that he was surrounded by traps, traps of every description, but particularly the cruel wire snares like those he had seen in the trap-line of death the day before.

A long-nosed Arab came out of the gloom rubbing his hands. 'You are interested in traps?'

'Very much interested,' Hal said. 'You sell these to poachers, don't you? Isn't that against the law?'

'The law,' laughed the Arab. 'In this country, now that the British have gone, we don't worry too much about the law. Do you run an operation?'

'What do you mean, an operation?'

'A poaching operation – like Blackbeard's.'

'So you know Blackbeard?'

'Of course. He's our best customer. We sell him a thousand snares at a time.'

'How much are they?'

'Well, the average snare requires two and a half yards of wire. The price is ten pence.'

'And a thousand snares – how many animals would they catch?'

'It depends on the season. And every operator has his own figures. Now, take Blackbeard – he estimates that from January to July each snare should take four animals a month. For a thousand snares, that's 28,000. During the dry season, August to October, only one a month. That's 3,000. During the big migration season, November and December, ten a month for each snare, and that's 20,000. Total for the year, 51,000.'

'Big business,' said Hal.

'The biggest business in the country,' the Arab said proudly.

'How do the animals like it?'

The Arab looked startled. 'Don't tell me you're one of those animal-lovers.' His face turned purple with anger. 'You've just been leading me on, haven't you? Get out of this shop before I throw you out.'

Farther down the street, Hal paused again. From the doorway came a musty, leathery smell that reminded him of the piles of hides and heads at the poachers' camp.

Entering, he found himself in a large warehouse that reached as far back as he could see. On each side it was piled from floor to ceiling with heads of lions, leopards, cheetahs, giraffes, buffaloes, zebras, wildebeests, rhinos, elephants, hippos, and antelopes; also tails by the thousand, elephants' feet hollowed to make waste-paper baskets or umbrella stands, rich stores of great ivory tusks, rhino horns beyond number, stuffed monkeys of every sort, and hides of everything from elephants to bush-babies.

The proprietor was an Indian. Hal picked up the beautiful antlered head of a Tommy gazelle.

'How much?' he asked.

'In what quantity?'

'How much for this head?'

'I'm sorry, sir, we can't sell you one only. We don't sell retail – just wholesale.'

'You mean, by the dozen, or by the gross?'

The Indian smiled. 'No, no. We don't deal in such small amounts. Our minimum order would be for about ten thousand specimens. In fact we usually sell by the shipload. We outfitted three ships yesterday. They're sailing this morning.'

'Where from?'

'The Old Harbour. Just down at the end of this street.'

Mombasa's 'Old Harbour', nestling among the coral cliffs at the north-east corner of the island, was full of large high-pooped Arab dhows. Those ready to leave were easily picked out, for their great lateen sails had already been raised and were idly flapping in the breeze.

A dark-skinned Arab who looked every inch a pirate stood by the gangway of the biggest dhow.

'Are you the captain of this ship?' Hal asked.

The man nodded.

Hal looked up admiringly at the great sweep of sail. He pulled out his camera.

'May I?'

The captain nodded again. Hal took the picture.

'Where are you off to?' he asked.

'Bombay.'

'A fine looking ship,' Hal said. 'I could get a better shot at that sail from the deck. Do you mind?'

The captain waved his hand towards the deck. Hal and Roger went aboard. Hal took a couple more pictures. He turned to find the captain beside him. Hal took his picture and the piratical face lighted with a smile.

'Do you speak English?' Hal asked.

'Pretty good.'

'What are you taking to Bombay?'

Hal did not expect an honest answer. But the captain evidently had no fear of possible spies, plain-clothes police, or customs officials.

'I show you.'

He lifted the edge of a tarpaulin so it was possible to see below deck. The great hold was crammed to the limit with the same sort of specimens that the boys had just seen in the warehouse. The dark face beamed with pride.

'Good, no?'

'All of these – how many?'

The captain pulled out his bill of lading. The number of trophies of each kind was set down. The grand total of all specimens was 180,000.

And this was but one of three vessels to sail in a single day, all chock full of trophies representing the death of thousands of Africa's animals.

'I can't understand it,' said the warden after Hal had made his report concerning the trial of the forty-seven poachers. 'Why Sindar was so easy on them baffles me. Perhaps it's just because he's so tender-hearted – can't bear to hurt either animal or man.' He dismissed the matter as if it were too painful and puzzling to think about.

'Anyhow,' he said, 'I have another plane trip mapped out for you. But this time I'd like you to take two passengers. One is a colobus and the other is an okapi. Come over to the hospital and I'll introduce you to them.'

17

Thirty million years old

THE animal hospital was alive with the grunts, groans, squeals, and squawks of everything from baby elephant to crowned crane.

'Meet the most beautiful monkey in all Africa,' said Crosby. 'This is the colobus.'

Truly it was handsome. It was pitch black and snow white. The rich black hair on its back contrasted with the flowing robes of white on its flanks and the picture-frame of white that encircled its black face.

'Its coat is gorgeous,' Hal said.

'Yes,' agreed the warden. 'And that may mean the death of it. The fur is in great demand for women's garments. High prices are paid for it, so the poachers are hot on the trail of the few colobus monkeys that are left. If something isn't done to stop the poaching, the finest of the monkeys will soon be as extinct as the dodo.'

'What a tail,' exclaimed Roger, looking at the great white bushy plume that restlessly fanned the air. 'Why, it must be longer than the monkey.'

'You're right,' replied Crosby. 'The body is usually about thirty-two inches long, and the tail forty inches.'

'What do you want us to do with it?' Hal asked.

'Take it where it will be safe. If we turn it loose here it will soon be picked up again by poachers. It doesn't belong here. How it ever got here I don't know. Colobus monkeys do best in a higher altitude than this. There are some of them left in the Aberdare Mountains – they feel at home there in the very tall trees and the cool mountain air, and they are pretty safe. So it would be fine if you could fly this one up to the Aberdares.'

'Okay. Is it ready to travel?'

'It got a nasty cut on the neck from the wire snare but we've treated it and I'm sure it will heal.'

'How will it like being cooped up in the plane?'

'I don't know. It depends on whether it trusts you or not. You both seem to have a way with animals, so I think you'll get along all right.'

The colobus cocked its picture frame face to one side and studied the boys with its soft brown eyes. It raised one hand and stroked its white beard.

'No thumb,' exclaimed Roger. 'I thought all monkeys had thumbs.'

'Practically all do. The colobus is an exception. It's a very intelligent animal, but it can't do what many other monkeys can do since it has no thumb. Do you realize how important the thumb is? Try picking things up without using it. You would have a lot of trouble using any sort of tool if you had no thumb. Man is very lucky because Nature gave him one. Much of our civilization is built round the thumb. Now come over here and meet your other passenger.'

He led the way to a cage occupied by an animal about the size of a mule. But it didn't look like a mule, nor like any animal the boys had ever seen.

'You're looking,' said the warden, 'at the rarest of all African animals. The okapi.'

'I've always wanted to see one,' Hal said. 'The okapi is listed at ten thousand dollars. Now I can see why it's worth so much.'

Every inch of the animal was different from every other inch. It was dabbed with colours as if an artist had brushed it with every paint he owned. It was yellow, red, chestnut, black, white, blue-black, maroon, sepia, cream, orange, and purple. All the colours blended perfectly in the wonderfully soft, glossy coat.

It seemed to be a combination of zebra, giraffe, and antelope. It had the head and short horns of a giraffe, the stripes of a zebra on its hindquarters, the large broad ears of a wild dog, and it seemed to wear white stockings.

Suddenly it looked like an ant-eater when it put out its tongue a foot long and licked itself behind the ears!

'It's a stranger here,' Crosby said. 'Like the colobus. It will certainly get killed if it stays here. It belongs in the deepest, darkest jungle in the northern Congo, or close to it. No white man knew it existed until sixty years ago. The pygmies knew about it and told white hunters about it but no one believed them. I wonder how many other animals there are hidden away in the jungle that we know nothing about. The okapi is very shy. He never came out and showed himself. He hid for thirty million years.'

Roger wrinkled his forehead. 'Did you say thirty million?'

'Naturalists know now that the species is that old. The

okapi has been called a living fossil. Most animals change, grow larger, or smaller, or become extinct. The okapi has stayed the same all that time. But now the poachers are after him and the chances are that very soon this thirty-million-year-old beauty will disappear.'

'Where can we take him where he'll be safe?'

'Nowhere,' said Crosby gloomily. 'Nowhere will be safe. But there is a place that the poachers haven't found yet and perhaps won't for a while. It's a big island in Lake Victoria. It's called Rubondo. It has fifty-five thousand acres of dense forest – just the kind the okapi loves. It has been set aside as a game sanctuary and it is protected by waters that can get very wild and stormy and poachers who try to get there are apt to be drowned. You could be drowned too. There's no airfield on the island. You would have to bring your plane down on the mainland and then charter a boat or raft to take you and the okapi over to the island. Perhaps you'd rather not try it.'

'It doesn't sound too bad,' said Hal. 'I suppose it would only take an hour or so to ferry across to the island.'

Crosby smiled. 'More than that. Victoria is the second largest lake in the world. Your voyage to the island would take fifteen hours. And if you didn't have about five storms on the way I'd be much surprised. I can't ask you to take the risk – it's up to you.'

'We'll go,' Hal said. 'If you'll show us how to get there.'

Back in the office, Crosby spread out the map of East Africa.

18

The treehouse

'THE Aberdares are here, north of Nairobi. You land at Nyeri, then trek in to Treetops. You've heard of Treetops?'

'Of course. The hotel perched in the top branches of a giant Cape chestnut.'

'Most of the forest trees there are giants. The colobus will love them. Stay overnight up in the treehouse. The next morning, fly three hundred miles south-west to Mwanza on Lake Victoria. Here it is. And there's Rubondo Island, a hundred miles across the lake.'

'When do we leave?'

'If you want to leave now, you can make Treetops before dark.'

'Let's go,' said Roger.

The animal passengers were not quite so enthusiastic. The two rear seats of the plane were removed to make room for them. The okapi in a close-fitting bamboo cage was driven to the landing field and five men hoisted the animal aboard.

'Won't he be too heavy for the plane?' Roger wondered.

'No,' said the warden. 'You have a 250-horsepower engine there. It will lift two and a half tons. That okapi can't weigh more than a quarter of a ton.'

The zebra-giraffe-antelope had never been in a spot like this in all his thirty million years. He whinnied like a worried horse and banged his head about against the bamboo slats, which bent when they were struck, so they did him no harm.

Crosby stripped a leafy branch from a tree and laid it on top of the cage so that the leaves hung down between the slats. The okapi at once coiled a twelve-inch ribbon of tongue round the leaves and drew them down within reach of the grinding teeth. So long as he had his favourite food, he could tolerate his strange environment.

The mild-mannered colobus did not need to be caged. Roger climbed into the plane with the monkey in his arms. With the curiosity natural to an intelligent animal, it examined the instrument board closely, then climbed back over Roger's shoulder to the top of the okapi's cage from which point it made a close examination of every inch of the cabin. When the engine began to roar it plopped back into Roger's lap and peered about anxiously as the plane thundered up over the treetops.

Hal followed the red road north-west to Nairobi, then turned north towards the dazzling snows of 17,000-foot Mount Kenya. Helped by a tail wind, he made the three-hundred-mile flight in two hours, then came down on a small but open landing field at the edge of the Aberdare forest.

Here was the Outspan Hotel where arrangements

must be made to enter the game reserve and spend the night at Treetops.

They had scarcely touched the ground when they were greeted by the hotel's white hunter who introduced himself with 'Call me Geoffrey'.

The okapi was left in the plane with plenty of leaves for supper and breakfast.

'He'll be all right there,' said Geoffrey. 'We'll look after him. Now, if you'll climb into this jeep, we'll be off.'

With Roger holding the colobus, the car slithered over a muddy forest trail for three miles, then came to a stop at the end of the road. Great trees towered all about.

'Now we have a quarter-mile walk to Treetops,' said Geoffrey.

They followed a narrow track among the forest giants. The colobus was getting more and more excited. These tall trees offered it an ideal home. The air cooled by the snows of Mount Kenya was bound to please an animal with a coat of fur so warm and thick.

'What's that ladder for?' asked Roger, noticing a ladder nailed to a tree. Farther down the trail was another – and then another.

'I'm afraid you're going to find out right now,' said Geoffrey. 'Quick – climb that ladder.'

'Why?'

'No time for questions and answers. Get up there fast.'

Roger climbed, the colobus clinging to his shoulder. Close behind came Hal and Geoffrey. There was a crashing sound in the forest, then five loudly trumpeting elephants came charging out of the gloom.

'Higher,' shouted Geoffrey.

They climbed until Roger reached the end of the ladder. The upstretched trunks of the elephants did not quite touch Geoffrey's feet.

'Now you know what the ladders are for,' said Geoffrey. 'I should have explained – it's a rule of this trail. Climb eight feet high in case of rhino or buffalo, eighteen feet if it's an elephant.'

'Are they really so savage?'

'The rhinos and buffaloes can be. You never know about the elephant. He may be just trying to tease you – or he may mean business. If some poacher has pinged him with an arrow, he will revenge himself on any human he happens to see.'

'What do we do now?'

'Just wait.'

'How long?'

'It may be five minutes, it may be five hours. You can't hurry an elephant. They'll go when they're ready.'

It was not the most comfortable place to wait, thought Roger – clinging to a ladder with a heavy monkey glued to your shoulder.

The elephants were in no hurry. They put in their time tearing up bushes and swallowing them, leaves, twigs, roots, and all. They glanced up now and then to make sure their quarry was still there.

The colobus was getting restless. It threw back its head and stared upwards. Gradually Roger realized that there was something alive above him. He looked up and could see nothing at first but a little movement of the leaves at the top of the tree.

Then he saw a face peering down. It was a black face with a white ring all about it. It must belong to a colobus monkey. Other faces like it appeared. The animals chattered down an invitation for Roger's colobus to come and join them.

'Shall I let it go?' Roger asked Geoffrey.

'This is as good a place as any,' said Geoffrey. 'The colobus monkeys are a very friendly sort. They'll give your friend the red-carpet treatment I'm sure.'

Roger was already fond of this gentle creature, but knew it would be better off with its own kind.

Hanging on with one hand, he used the other to shift the animal over on to a branch beside his head. The colobus sat on the branch and looked long and thoughtfully at Roger. Then it climbed up branch by branch to the welcoming party above. There was a new burst of happy talk when it arrived and there was no doubt that the stranger had at once been adopted as a full member of the Aberdare colony.

'Don't look so blue,' said Geoffrey. 'You'll probably see it again. The monkeys come down to drink every night at the Treetops lake.'

The elephants had wandered off. The march to Treetops was resumed. Now they could see it through the trees, and it was a strange sight. A hotel floating in the air! It was perched fifty feet above the ground in the top branches of a big tree and it moved slightly backwards and forwards as the tree swayed in the wind. A wooden stairway something like a spider's web hung from the door down to the ground.

It was like a six-storey building with the lower five storeys removed. It was as if wreckers had destroyed all of a building for fifty feet up but had forgotten to take the top floor. There it seemed to float in the sky, defying the laws of gravity.

Directly in front of the hotel was a small lake completely surrounded by forest. The boys had heard much about this famous place. They knew that at night all sorts of animals came out of the forest to drink at the lake and root around in the mud for salt. You could look down on them from the balcony of the hotel and if you made no sound they would not be aware of your presence.

Many notable people had slept in this little hotel in the sky.

'Queen Elizabeth has been here, I believe,' Hal said.

'Yes – but she was Princess Elizabeth when she came. During the night she got word that her father the king had died and she was queen.'

'And Prince Philip?'

'He has visited us several times. Of course he is the strongest man we have in the whole movement for the protection of African wild life. Come along – we'll go upstairs.'

They approached the cobweb. The boys were surprised to find that the lowest twelve feet of it were missing – or, at least, these steps had been drawn up out of reach.

Geoffrey pressed a button and the steps came down. After they had climbed them, he pressed another button and up they went like the companion-way of a ship when it is about to sail.

'What's the idea?' Hal inquired.

'If they're not up out of the way the big animals will smash them or the small animals will climb them. So we hoist that section out of reach.'

'Like the drawbridge of a castle,' Hal said.

They climbed the rest of the steps to this castle in the clouds and entered the hotel door.

Geoffrey introduced them to the manager and they were assigned a room.

In comparison with most hotels, this one was tiny, accommodating only twelve guests – yet as a treehouse it was surprisingly large. It swayed when the tree swayed. If any guest stepped heavily the whole structure trembled.

Outside the boys' room was a balcony from which they could look straight down to the beach of the little lake. There was a stairway to the roof where one had an unobstructed view in all directions.

19

House of whispers

It was a house of whispers. Signs warned that any sound would disturb the game. The white hunter whispered, the guests whispered, the servants whispered. Everyone wore rubber-soled shoes. It was the rule. Tackies (tennis shoes) could be bought if you did not have a pair.

'But there's one thing I don't understand,' Hal said to Geoffrey. 'Even though the animals can't hear us, surely they can smell us. We're only fifty feet away.'

'If we were down on their level they would certainly get our scent – perhaps even if we were a quarter of a mile away. But here, fifty feet above them, the air currents carry our scent high above their heads. They don't know we exist – unless we make a noise. This is no place for a person with a cold. One cough, and all the animals scamper into the forest. But they come back. They love this place. The soil in that beach happens to be full of salt. All animals need salt – except the meat eaters. They get it from the meat they eat.'

An excellent dinner was served at the long table in the dining-room. Then every one of the twelve guests slipped out silently on to the balcony and sat to look down on the pageant below. All wore heavy clothing, and some had wrapped themselves in blankets stripped from their beds, for the mountain air at an altitude of seven thousand feet was cold in spite of the fact that Treetops was almost on the equator.

Darkness veiled the scene. But suddenly a powerful floodlight was turned on. It illuminated the beach and the edge of the lake. Two busy pigs, a wart-hog, and a stately waterbuck had already arrived. They looked up into the light. Perhaps they were surprised to see the sun shining at that hour of the night, but they were not frightened. They could not see the balcony and the spectators, for the hotel was now completely dark. They went back to their search for salt.

Four rhinos came on the scene. They eagerly sucked up the salty mud. Others joined them. They quarrelled over the choicest mudholes, pushed and jostled each other, made angry blowing sounds and a peculiar blast that sounded like a loud snore. Their ears went round like radar screens picking up signals. A slight cough of one of the guests sent them galumphing off.

Soon they were back, or others like them, chasing each other, making a puff-puff-puff like a steam locomotive. They also snorted like a horse, but with rhino power instead of horsepower.

Now came the elephants, great lumbering monsters, wading into the lake and throwing water up over their dusty hides, then coming out to insert the delicate tips of their trunks into deep footprints made by the rhinos. There they found salt and conveyed it to their mouths. They blinked now and then at the floodlight but evid-

ently took it for the moon or for a sun that had forgotten to set.

Unlike the hot-tempered rhinos, the elephants did not
interfere with each other. And when a baby elephant
poked its trunk into a hole already being explored by an
adult, the big one let the little fellow have it.

Five shaggy buffaloes now came on the stage and they
proved as hot-tempered as the rhinos. Soon the beach
was a battlefield where the weapons were rhino horns
against the harder, sharper horns of the buffaloes, and
the night resounded with their grunting and trumpeting.

The elephants didn't like the squabble and finally all
joined in a screaming charge that sent the misbehavers
flying into the forest.

A giraffe came out to drink. He had to spread his legs
far apart to get his head down to the water. The lake was
surrounded now by graceful antelopes of many sorts;
impalas, Tommies, Grant's, kudu, waterbuck, and klip-
springer. These charming and dainty animals took care
not to get under the feet of the monsters.

'Look. There they come,' whispered Roger.

The visitors both boys had been eagerly waiting for
slipped out of the forest into the light. They were the
colobus monkeys. What lovely creatures they were with
their white-ringed faces, their rich silky fur and magnificent white tails! No wonder they were so loved by
fashionable ladies that they were being slaughtered at
the rate of more than ten thousand a month.

Roger strained his eyes. Was his friend among them?
He borrowed a pair of binoculars from Geoffrey.

Yes – there was no mistake about it – he could make
out on the neck of one of them a line where the wire

noose had rubbed away the fur and cut into the flesh.

The trusting creature he had held on his lap seemed to be equally happy with its new friends. Roger felt a pang of jealousy but was instantly ashamed of it. The pretty creature that might have made such a good pet was where it belonged, with others of its own sort, and among the great trees it loved.

The boys kept vigil most of the night – then returned to their cots to dream of what they had seen.

At breakfast Hal said to Geoffrey, 'What a wonderful idea it was – to build a treehouse over this pool.'

Geoffrey agreed. 'Only a person with a good imagination would have thought of it. It was a woman, you know. A certain Lady Bettie Walker came here with friends long before this was made a National Park. She had been reading *Swiss Family Robinson*. You remember the treehouse described in that book. That gave her the idea for Treetops. It seemed a crazy idea to some of her friends.'

'Crazy or not, it's great. I hate to leave but we'd better be getting along. We have a big day ahead.'

Back to the plane and the patient okapi, nibbling a leafy breakfast. The flight over the great lion country of the Serengeti Plain to Mwanza on the south shore of Lake Victoria took two hours.

There, Hal chartered the only craft available, a clumsy raft with a wheezy outboard motor, and set out on the fifteen-hour passage to Rubondo Island.

Warden Crosby's prediction that there would be five storms during the fifteen hours proved wrong. There was only one storm – but it lasted fifteen hours.

A strong north wind sweeping down the 250-mile length of the mighty lake brought big waves that washed across the raft, sousing boys and okapi alike. The boys were not allowed to forget that among all the freshwater lakes of the world only Superior is greater than Victoria. This lake deserved to be named after England's great queen and had all the majesty one had a right to expect of the source of the mighty Nile.

The okapi had certainly never made such a trip before and whinnied his strong disapproval. The constant tossing of the raft made the animal seasick and up came the leaves. The cage had been firmly lashed to the logs, yet the force of the waves against it seemed about to tear it loose at any moment.

Victoria is a lake of hidden reefs, lying just below the surface. Time and again the raft stumbled to a halt on a sand-bar. Sometimes reversing the engine would back it off. Sometimes this was not good enough and the boys must jump off and push the raft free. If on these occasions a six-foot wave came along and completely buried you, that was just part of the game.

One must keep a sharp look out for the crocodiles and hippos that infest the lake. Several times there was a wild scramble back on to the logs as the swish of a great tail signalled the approach of a croc. The hippos did not like the storm water and lurked in the lee of small islands. Not being carnivores, they preferred reeds to humans as their diet – nevertheless they were dangerous as the boys found out when one came up beneath the raft, hoisting it three feet into the air before it slid off edgewise into the water. Whether the great beast performed this feat just for fun, or with evil intent, the navigators did not stop to ask. They merely congratulated themselves that the raft had not been turned upside down.

The troubles of the day became a nightmare as darkness settled on the wild waters of the lake. A light far ahead marked Rubondo Island. Sometimes it disappeared entirely behind rain and mist. Then only guesswork steered the raft. After a time the light would reappear off one quarter or the other and the course could be corrected.

Three exhausted sailors finally brought their craft into a fairly quiet cove of Rubondo and heard a welcoming shout from the wharf.

The warden, who introduced himself with 'Just call me Tony', helped them put the cage ashore. 'What have you got in there?'

'An okapi.'

'Wonderful. Male or female?'

It seemed an odd question. What did it matter?

'Male,' Hal said.

'Good. We have just one okapi on the island and it's a female. Now we have a chance of breeding more. Mighty rare animal, the okapi. You can be sure we'll handle this one with kid gloves. Wait till I get a towel.'

He ran to his small rustic cabin and came back with a towel. It was not for the shivering boys, but to dry the precious okapi. The cage was cautiously opened and the animal brought out on to the wharf.

Tony went over every inch of the hide with the towel, rubbing briskly to stimulate circulation. 'There – he'll do,' said Tony finally.

'Should we feed him?' said Hal.

'No need. He can't go ten feet in these woods without finding food. And as for water, he has a whole lake of it.'

'So we just let him go?' inquired Roger, always sorry to lose a pet.

'That's the best thing for him. Just let him make his own way. He'll be pretty safe. He has no enemies on this island – no lions, leopards, or poachers. A good many rhinos have been brought here for safe keeping, but they

won't bother your okapi. This is as close to heaven as any okapi will ever get.'

The okapi was already eagerly moving off into his heaven.

Hal had a pang of regret as he saw ten thousand dollars walking away. He and Roger had been sent to Africa to get animals for their animal-collector father who would then sell them to zoos. It seemed a pity to lose this one. But Hal was aware that few okapi had ever survived the journey to America. The important thing right now was not to capture an animal or two for their father, but to do everything possible to stop the killing of the thousands of animals of East Africa. In the long run that would do more for their business of animal-collecting than anything else they could do.

'Now,' said Tony, 'come along to the cabin. It's your turn to get dry – and you must be starved.'

20

Men live, animals die

THE night was half gone before the boys were dried, fed and bunked in Tony's cabin.

Roger was asleep in two minutes. Hal lay awake a little longer, worrying about the trip back – fifteen hours over the stormy lake, then two hours by plane. Impossible to get to Tsavo before dark. Impossible to come down on that tiny landing strip after dark.

Then he slept and did not wake until roused by the sizzle and smell of bacon and eggs. Tony had some good news for him.

'I'm going to take you back to Mwanza in our launch. It will cut the time from fifteen hours down to seven. The boys can take the raft back later. There's just one condition.'

'What's that?'

'That you give me a lift to Tsavo. I have some matters to discuss with Crosby – about a shipment of four rhinos to Rubondo.'

The hundred-mile dash to Mwanza by launch was pure joy compared with the painful and dangerous voyage by raft. By mid-afternoon they were aboard the Stork and flying again over the mysterious Serengeti Plain.

'See that deep cut in the plain? Looks like the Grand Canyon. Fly low over it.'

Hal flew low. He was trying to remember what he had heard about this canyon.

'Is it Olduvai Gorge?'

Tony turned to him in surprise. 'So, you know about Dr Leakey. With luck, we may see him and his crew at work.'

Hal followed the twists and turns of the gorge. Then suddenly, straight below, could be seen a group of men at the bottom of the gorge digging into the rock wall.

The whirr of the plane made them look up. They waved and Tony waved back. Then they were left behind. It had been only a moment, but a moment Hal would always remember. For that single glance had carried his imagination back two million years.

Roger, who had never heard of Olduvai, was not impressed.

'What's so wonderful about that hole in the ground?' he wanted to know.

Tony explained. 'This archaeologist, Dr Leakey, has been digging there for several years. He had found the fossil bones of men who lived two million years ago. Those are the oldest human bones that have ever been discovered anywhere in the world.'

'How can they tell they're that old?'

'A chemical test. Perhaps you've heard of the Carbon 14 test. That's been used for a long time – the only trouble with it is that it can't tell the age of anything more than fifty thousand years old. But there's a new method now, the potassium-argon test. With that they can go back millions of years.'

'And this two-million-year-old man – was he like man today?'

'Apparently he was. Dr Leakey has found the bones of sixteen men. They were all pretty much like ours, but with some differences. Those men were only about four feet tall. Their thumbs and fingers were not as well adapted as ours for picking things up and holding them. Still they could use tools – some of their stone tools were found. The weight of these men was only about half the weight of modern man – five stone five pounds instead of ten stone ten. The weight of the brain was only one pound. Modern man's brain weight is about three pounds. So, you see, man really has improved a bit during the last two million years.'

'The thing that strikes me as remarkable,' said Hal, 'is that we have lasted that long. Think of all the animals that have died out during that time – the mastodon, brontosaurus, diplodocus, dodo, quagga, moa, and hundreds of others. All gone. And we go merrily along – not only still living, but multiplying to beat the band.'

'Multiplying too fast,' Tony said. 'And the faster we multiply, the faster we push the remaining animals off the planet. We seem to think we own everything. How about our fellow-animals – don't they have any rights?'

They passed over one of the greatest of the world's craters, with one of the strangest of names, Ngorongoro. The volcanic fires had long since died out. The surrounding rim of the crater stood up like a wall two thousand five hundred feet above the crater floor. The floor was a lush green expanse of a hundred and fifty square miles, dotted with woods and meadows and lakes and swarming with animals.

'Lots of life here,' Roger remarked.

'Yes, but what kind of life? Let's get down a little closer.'

Flying lower, they could see dozens of lions, elephants, rhinos – but most of the room was taken up by thousands upon thousands of cattle tended by tall, bare Masai herdsmen.

'This is the beginning of the end of this heaven for wild animals,' Tony said. 'It used to be reserved for them. But now the Masai have invaded it and their cattle are crowding out the wild life. The Masai have no need for so many cattle – they keep them just to show off. The same thing is happening in the national parks, even in Tsavo. Herds of bony, scrawny, worthless cattle are driving out the wild life.'

The crater was left behind and Lake Manyara appeared – a curiously pink lake, for on its surface rested millions of pink flamingoes.

'At least the lake is safe from the cattle,' said Hal.

'Yes, but the flamingoes are having a different kind of problem. This lake has become very salty. The salt hardens on the flamingoes' legs and makes great heavy balls three or four inches thick so that the birds cannot walk or fly. They starve to death by the tens of thousands.'

'Is anything being done about it?'

'Something fine is being done. See all those African youngsters down there wading among the flamingoes? They have been trained to save the birds by breaking up

the ball of salt with a hammer so that the leg is once more clean and free.'

'So African children really do care?'

'Yes. I only wish their parents cared as much.'

A strong blast of snow-cold air struck the plane as it passed the glaciers of Mount Kilimanjaro. Then Hal brought it down skilfully on the Tsavo strip.

They found Mark Crosby at his desk. The two Englishmen, Tony and Mark, greeted each other heartily.

'Nice to see there's a bit of England left in Kenya,' said Tony. 'I rather expected that by this time I'd see an African behind that desk.'

Crosby laughed. 'It will happen one of these days. Now that this country has its own government, official jobs like yours and mine will sooner or later be given to Africans.'

'Are you going to wait for it to happen? Or resign now?'

'I'll wait. For two reasons. One is that there's no African yet with enough training to take over my job. The other reason is personal. I'd rather take my chances here than face going back to England. What would I do there? I couldn't get a job. They'd ask me, "What experience have you had?" "Well, I've been a game warden in Africa." What use is that in England?'

Hal thought that both men looked tired. They faced an uncertain future. They had given their lives to saving the wild life of Africa. Would all they had done go for nothing? It was only natural for an African government to give important posts to Africans. But would Africans care as much about protecting the wild life? For hundreds of years they had been used to killing animals, not protecting them. Would the national parks be split up into farms for the rapidly increasing African population? Was there no way that people and animals could live together in peace? Hal could almost see these thoughts running like a motion picture through the minds of the two Englishmen.

'Well,' said Tony, 'we can't moon around about what may be. We can only do the best we can right now. I understand you have four rhinos ready for Rubondo. I'll see them through. I'll need a cage for each animal, and two lorries. I'll take them by road to Mwanza, and I've chartered an old car-ferry for the trip to the island.'

While the two wardens discussed the transfer of the rhinos, Hal and Roger went to their banda. They found a note wedged under the door. Hal unfolded it and read it aloud.

'GO HOME, YANKS. THIS IS YOUR FIRST WARNING. IF ANOTHER IS NEEDED IT WILL BE WRITTEN IN BLOOD – YOURS.'

Bb

'Somebody playing cops and robbers,' said Roger contemptuously.

Hal did not take it so lightly. 'I have an idea he means it. You know who it is, don't you?'

Roger studied the signature, Bb.

'I can guess,' he said. 'Blackbeard.'

'Right. Don't brush it off. He's a man who would go to any limit, even murder, to save a business that is bringing him in millions.'

'So you think we should go home?' said Roger sarcastically.

'No. Not until we get done with Bb. You remember that five-mile trap-line we saw from the plane? We'll go after it tomorrow morning.'

'But what's the use? We nab a gang of poachers and send them to court and the judge lets them off.'

'This time we'll try to nab Blackbeard, not his poachers. But we'll give them a surprise too – something they won't like. Perhaps it will make them think twice before they do any more poaching.'

21

Tear gas

'WE'LL be turning in early,' Hal told the warden after reporting the delivery of the colobus to Treetops and the okapi to Rubondo.

'Good idea,' said Crosby. 'It was a hard trip. Thanks for doing a good job.'

'Tomorrow morning we want to visit that trap-line we saw from the plane. We'll make another try to grab Blackbeard.'

'Fine. Sorry I can't go with you. I certainly wish you the best of luck.'

After they were in bed they heard a car drive up. Before they got up at dawn they heard a car drive away. They thought nothing of this coming and going until later.

After a sunrise breakfast the boys and their crew set out in jeeps and Land-Rovers for the trap-line. When they came within a mile of it Hal brought the cars to a halt and gave the men final instructions.

'You will find canisters of tear gas in the supply truck. Each of you take one.' He went on to explain carefully the plan of attack.

The cars rumbled on. When they arrived at the trap-line they drew up in front of it just as they had done before. They blew their horns lustily to attract the poachers. But as the poachers began to come out through the gaps in the trap-line, Hal led a dozen of his men round through the woods to come up on the poachers' camp from the rear.

If Blackbeard behaved as he had before, he would stay safely behind his men and, when he saw them being defeated, he would try to sneak out the back way. But this time he would find himself trapped.

On the front line, arrows began to fly. The safari men did not fire back but stayed behind the barricade of cars.

The poachers grew bolder. Shouting insults at the men who seemed afraid to come out and fight, they came closer. The safari men looked to Roger for a signal.

When the poachers were within fifty feet Roger threw his canister and at once the air was full of the bombs which burst among the animal-killers upon striking rocks or the hard ground. Within seconds the poachers could hardly be seen amid the clouds of yellow-white tear gas. Choking, suffocating, weeping, they fell over each other in their mad rush to escape. They squirmed on the ground, and buried their faces in the grass. Some staggered back towards the camp. No arrows were flying now.

At the same moment Hal's men rushed in from the rear among the grass huts and into the gaps in the trap-line looking for Blackbeard. He was nowhere to be seen. Nor was there any sign of his boot-prints. The search was continued for half an hour, but without any results.

By this time some of the poachers were able to stand,

but still could hardly see through their tears. All the fight had been taken out of them. They waited to be loaded into cars and transported to Mombasa.

But if they hoped to spend a few days resting in jail, they were disappointed.

'Tell them,' Hal said to Joro, 'to go back to their villages and stay there. Tell them if they are caught poaching again something worse will happen to them.'

All the animals still alive in the snares were set free; some were taken to the hospital, the dead were left to the hyenas and jackals. The wire snares were collected, and all the trophies, some of them very valuable, some very odd.

Among the odd ones were bracelets made from the hairs of elephants' tails, and leopards' whiskers which had been gathered to sell to African witch doctors. When mixed with a drink and swallowed, the sharp, stiff little hairs pierced the walls of the stomach and caused death.

The grass shacks and the five-mile barricade of thorn bushes were burned to the ground.

Back at the lodge, Hal told Crosby the unhappy story. Blackbeard had not been caught.

'Never mind,' the warden said. 'You destroyed the camp, and you scared the poachers. That's something. As for Blackbeard, you'll get him yet. By the way, Judge Singh wishes you luck.'

'Was he here?'

'He drove in last night after you had turned in. He left very early this morning – said he had important business.'

'Did you tell him where we were going this morning?'

'Of course. He is always interested in these raids. He is very happy about the fine work you are doing.'

Hal hesitated. 'Warden, I hate to say this, because I know the judge is a personal friend of yours – but I've begun to wonder whether he is really with us or against us.'

The remark took Crosby by surprise. He stared at Hal.

'That is a very strange thing to say about a man who has always been one of the chief supporters of the anti-poaching campaign. Of course he's a personal friend of mine. You remember, he saved my life. He's also a friend of the wild life. He never fails to speak up against poaching.'

'Does he just talk? Or does he really do something?'

'He really does something.'

Crosby opened a drawer of his desk and took out a cheque. He laid it before Hal. 'The judge gave me this last night. I will send it on to the treasurer of the Wildlife Society.'

The cheque was for two hundred pounds. It was made out to the African Wildlife Society and it was signed Sindar Singh.

'You see,' Crosby said, 'he does more than talk. In this country a judge's salary is very small. Two hundred pounds represents a real sacrifice for him. Now, do you doubt his sincerity?'

'I'm sorry,' said Hal. 'Perhaps I'm wrong.'

'I am sure you are,' Crosby said with a touch of severity.

Hal returned to his banda. He told Roger about the conversation and the cheque.

'He certainly caught me flat-footed,' Hal confessed. 'Perhaps we've been mistaken all along.'

Roger was not ready to give in. 'I still think he's a crook.'

'Then how do you explain that cheque?'

'Simple enough. If he's really mixed up in this racket he isn't living on a judge's salary. He's making millions on the side. To him, two hundred pounds is nothing. It's just to pull the wool over the warden's eyes and make the society think he's on their side. I still think he's Blackbeard's buddy.'

'You think so and I think so, but we can never convince the warden. We'd better give up trying. If we keep on, we'll only get him down on us. First we must get some real evidence.'

'I guess we can't prove anything yet,' Roger admitted. 'But we're sure getting some evidence. There was that funny business about the Aco. If you hadn't stopped Singh, the warden would be dead now. And those silly sentences in court. And that warning signed Bb. How do you suppose it got here? I'll bet a plugged nickel Judge Singh brought it from Blackbeard.'

Hal nodded. 'Could be,' he said, 'And today we didn't find Blackbeard at the poachers' camp. Why not? Perhaps he'd been warned. The warden told the judge last night what we were planning to do. The judge left very early this morning. Perhaps he stopped at the poachers' hangout and tipped off Blackbeard.' Hal brushed his hand wearily across his forehead. 'But these are all perhapses. We've got to get some real proof.'

'Well, we won't get it sitting round here. Let's go.'

22

Massacre

TWICE they had spotted camps from the air. It was worth trying again.

In the Stork they flew over hill and valley, scanning the ground through binoculars.

They looked for another trap-line. A trap-line would be a dead give-away. It was a sure sign of poachers, and easy to see.

But there was no trap-line. No camp of grass huts. No spearmen or bowmen searching for animals. Mile after mile, no sign of human life.

'Perhaps we've scared them off,' Roger said.

'No such luck. Perhaps they're just hiding in the woods.'

'Swing over to that waterhole.'

It was solid with animals – elephants, rhinos, zebras, everything under the sun. But no poachers.

Suddenly the waterhole blew up in a mighty fountain of spray and smoke that reminded them of Old Faithful. The explosion made the plane bounce and stagger. Small animals and torn-off parts of large ones were shot into the sky. What had a moment ago been a source of cool

refreshment for hundreds of creatures was now their grave.

'Dynamite,' Hal exclaimed.

Out of the woods poured the poachers, spearing animals that were still alive, chopping off tails, horns, heads, anything that would bring a price.

Suddenly they saw the plane, and ran for cover. Hal circled and flew back at full speed to the lodge.

There he lost no time in mobilizing his men and their vehicles but, hurry as they might, it was nearly an hour before they could get through to the dynamited waterhole.

They were too late. The poachers had taken all they wanted and made good their escape.

The mangled corpses of animals filled the waterhole. If they were allowed to remain there they would rot and poison the water.

Hal's men with the help of a few rangers worked long and hard at cleaning out the spring. At nightfall they returned to the lodge, blue and moody. Roger expressed what they all felt:

'A tough day, and what have we got for it? One big fat nothing.'

Early morning found the two scouts aloft once more. This time their flight took them far to the north, forty miles, fifty, sixty, but still over the wilderness of Tsavo Park. Then, another ten miles farther north, they saw a column of smoke.

Coming closer, they could see a milling madhouse of several hundred elephants surrounded by a ring of fire.

The poachers were at a safe distance. The elephant-grass in this plain was twelve feet high – they had set it on fire in a great circle round the elephant herd, and all they had to do was to wait for the animals to be roasted alive.

The crazed beasts charged into the roaring flames in a last desperate effort to escape and were so severely burned that they died lingering deaths of agony. Those that did not perish at once danced about curiously, because the soles of their feet had been burned away. Even if they should escape the flames they would not escape death, for they could not travel in search of food on the burned stumps of feet. They would soon be overtaken by poachers and killed.

Among the bare-skinned black poachers the boys could make out a black-bearded white face above a bush jacket and safari trousers.

'That's Blackbeard,' Roger exclaimed.

They swept close to take a look. Blackbeard glanced up, smiled, and waved.

'The devil!' Hal said. 'He knows he's safe. Before we could get back here with the trucks he could be a hundred miles away.'

They did get back with the trucks, but it was as they had feared. The poachers had taken all they had time to collect and had fled.

The boys had failed again. But it was not a complete failure. In their haste the poachers had left behind the most valuable trophies.

They had had time to remove such items as tails, feet, eyelashes, and some of the great ears – which would stiffen and could be used as table tops. But they had been in such a hurry to be off that they had left behind the most valuable parts – the tusks.

There is no quick and easy way to remove an elephant's tusk. It is strongly rooted in the great beast's bone and flesh. To chop it out with an axe is an almost superhuman task. The easiest method is to allow the carcass to decay for a week – then the tusk can be worked loose.

But it must have been evident to Blackbeard that he was not going to be allowed a week. In less than three hours the interfering strangers would be back with their cars and men. A few of the tusks had been chopped out but more than ninety per cent of them remained. It must have been a sore disappointment for the poacher chief to have to leave behind a store of ivory that would have added perhaps a hundred thousand dollars to his illegal loot.

The killer king's operations became more secretive. He and his poacher army seemed to have vanished. The Stork scouted hill and dale, forest and plain, without spotting a single trespasser. There were no more traplines, no more explosions, no more fires. There were no more camps of grass shacks. Perhaps there were no more poachers.

'Do you think we've really frightened them off?' Roger wondered.

'No. But I don't understand where they can be. It's almost as if they had gone underground.'

Underground. It made Roger think. He remembered his own experience underground, in the elephant pit.

Had the poachers dug themselves in? Tomorrow he would keep an eye open for brush-covered pits.

Back at the lodge the boys found Singh.

'Well, my friends, have you caught your man yet?'

'Not yet.'

'If I were you I'd give it up. We've been trying for years to get hold of him. But he's just too smart for us. In some ways I must say I admire him. The way he slips through your fingers is quite amazing, don't you think? But of course you'll get him yet. You Americans are so clever.'

Hal pretended not to see the hidden sarcasm in this remark.

The judge was evidently very well satisfied with himself. Hal encouraged his self-esteem.

'By the way,' he said, 'the warden told me of your contribution to the Wildlife Society. That was very generous of you.'

The judge smiled expansively and waved his hand. 'Nothing, my dear boy, nothing. I only wish it could have been more. Unfortunately, salaries are limited in my profession. But I am willing to do without some of the luxuries of life in order to help the poor dear animals.'

'Quite noble of you,' Hal said. 'Too bad you don't have any income besides your salary. Some judges make out quite well, you know.'

The judge's face darkened. 'Whatever do you mean?'

'Well, take a purely imaginary case. Suppose you were not such an honest and noble judge. Suppose you were secretly in the poaching racket. When any poachers came into your court you could let them off with little or no punishment. You could close your eyes to what the big operators are doing – and they would make it worth your while. You could become rich – and all the time you could pose as a great friend of the animals. And every once in a while you could make a gift to the Wildlife Society just to keep everybody fooled.'

The judge was flushing deeply and his usually soft eyes were like hard steel swordpoints. Then he forced a laugh.

'As you say, this is all purely imaginary,' he said. 'Quite impossible for a true lover of animals.'

'Quite,' agreed Hal, caressing Chee who had wandered in through the open door. Chee bared his teeth at the judge and snarled deeply.

Hal excused himself and went out. He looked back through a window screened with shrubbery. The judge's behaviour was remarkable. For the moment he seemed to have gone mad. He struck the desk a blow with his fist, then leaped up, strode backwards and forwards as if in a fever, came to where Chee was lying and gave the animal a vicious kick in the throat. Chee sprang up and came for him, spitting, biting, and clawing. Singh kicked the animal repeatedly, then drew a knife. Before he could use it, the wrist of the hand that held the knife was between the cheetah's teeth. The knife fell to the floor and the judge collapsed into a chair. Chee, still snarling, walked out.

Hal went to his banda and thought about what he had seen. So this was the great animal-lover! The cheetah evidently didn't think so and Hal trusted the animal more than the man. Hal was more convinced than ever that Sindar Singh was a colossal crook – otherwise why did he react so violently to Hal's 'purely imaginary' story?

But still there was no real proof.

23

Crash of the Stork

'I BELIEVE those are pits,' exclaimed Roger, looking down through the Perspex bubble.

Hal, at the controls, scanned the earth below. He could see no pits – but there were many spots where the brush had been cut and was now lying in mats, and those mats might be the covers of pits. Were poachers hidden beneath?

Near by was a grove of baobabs, fantastic trees that

looked like blown-up hippos. They were huge like hippos, bulged like hippos, had bark like the hide of a hippo. One might almost believe that a herd of the hefty animals had come up from the river and stood here until they took root.

There were none of the usual grass huts of poachers among the trees and not a sign of human life. Yet there was something suspicious about those brush mats. There might be a small city of busy men beneath them.

'It's worth investigating,' Hal said. He swung the plane about and headed home. 'We'll come back on wheels with our gang.'

For ten minutes the plane flew steadily on the homeward course. Then it began to weave and wobble as if it were drunk.

'Pockets!' guessed Roger.

'I don't think so,' Hal said. 'It's not bumping the way it would if it were dropping into air pockets. Besides, why should there be up-and-down air currents here? You might expect turbulence over bad country, hills, cliffs – but not over a level plain like this one.'

'Then what can it be? Are you wagging that stick?'

'Of course not.'

'Do you think the rudder has gone haywire?'

'I don't know. But it's getting worse every minute. I think we'd better look for a place to land.'

The plane was now bucking like a frightened horse.

'Your right wing,' exclaimed Roger. 'Look at it.'

The wing was dancing. It seemed about to come off and fly away on a trip of its own.

Hal brought the plane down in a steep glide. He

barely missed the top of a tall kapok tree. The plane rocked dangerously.

'I can't hold her,' Hal said. 'She's going to crash. She may burn. Be ready to jump clear.'

He turned off the ignition.

The plane struck the ground and bounced. There was a ripping, tearing sound, the right wing disappeared, the Stork crashed into an ant-hill and lay still.

'Good,' cried Hal.

'What's good about it?'

'No fire. We're alive. Isn't that good?'

'I suppose so,' Roger said doubtfully. 'What do we do now?'

They climbed out of the cabin and walked back fifty feet to inspect the torn-off wing.

'It doesn't seem possible,' said Hal. 'Why should that wing rip loose?'

Roger was inspecting the torn edge. 'Looks fishy to me,' he said. 'Did this just tear – or was it cut?'

Hal studied the break, then stared at Roger.

'Monkey business,' he exclaimed. 'See this straight line? That's no natural break. Somebody has sawed part of the way through – just enough to weaken the wing. I suppose we can feel honoured. Somebody thinks us important enough to be worth murdering.'

Roger was rubbing his knee. What's the matter?' Hal asked.

'Just a bump I got when we landed. Now what do we do? No radio in this crate. How about a signal fire?'

'No luck. The lodge is a good fifty miles away. They wouldn't see it. The only ones who would be likely to see it would be the poachers. And we don't want them to come down on us. A fire would be an open invitation to Mr Blackbeard.'

'Then what do we do? Just sit here and wait for somebody to come looking for us?'

'In a hundred miles of wild country? It might take weeks for them to find us. By that time we wouldn't be worth finding. There's only one way out of it. We've got to walk to the lodge.'

They went back to the plane. Hal noticed that Roger was limping badly. 'You'll never make it,' he said.

'Never mind the knee,' said Roger. 'It will limber up.'

'I'm afraid not. It will just get worse. Anyhow, one of us should stay here to look after the plane.'

'Why does it need looking after? What could happen to it?'

'Lots of things. A poacher might come on it and steal everything he could pry loose. Rhinos and elephants can get mighty curious. They completely wrecked a stalled plane up in Murchison a month ago. Hyenas have a taste for rubber – they'll eat the tyres off the wheels if you give them a chance. You can help most by staying right here.'

'Okay,' Roger said reluctantly. 'How long will it take you?'

'Assuming we're fifty miles from the lodge – I'd say it'll be a ten-hour walk. Then it'll take about two hours to get back here by truck. Twelve hours altogether.'

'But it's late afternoon already. You'd better wait until tomorrow morning.'

'Cooler walking at night,' Hal said. 'And there's a good moon. Don't worry – I'll get through all right. So long – take care of yourself. I'll be seeing you round about five a.m.'

He strode off. Roger's stomach called after him, 'Bring a sandwich back with you.'

As the sun went down the animals that had spent the heat of the day in the forest began to come out.

They were greatly interested in the plane. They gathered round it as if it had been the Ark and they were about to take a ride. Some of the smaller and more fearless ones tried to climb in with Roger. The baboons were determined to share the cabin with him. The vervet monkeys perching on the nose of the plane looked in through the Perspex.

Four rhinos looked the plane over carefully with many sniffs and snorts, perhaps thinking it was some new sort of beast. Then they retired to a short distance and held a conference.

They evidently decided that this strange creature had no business here. They lowered their heads and charged. Even one rhino could do serious damage to the fuselage. What might four do?

Roger threw open the hood and shouted. The rhinos stopped, blinking their weak eyes, tilting their ears to locate the source of the sound.

They held another conference. If they had been wise old elephants they might have reached an agreement. But being rhinos, irritable by nature and not very wise, they broke up the conference by fighting each other.

Gazelles and giraffes paraded round the plane examining it carefully. The famous jumpers, the impalas, had great fun leaping over it. A lurking leopard selected a waterbuck as its evening meal and broke its neck in one violent attack.

A terrifying scream ripped the air. It was loud enough and strong enough to come from a bull elephant – but Roger, when he got over the chill it gave him, remembered that it was just the night cry of the tree hyrax, a nocturnal animal only a foot or so long.

He was sorry to see the light go. The plane was left in shadow, and the shadow was climbing up the slope of Africa's highest mountain. Now it was a mile high, now two miles, now it reached the snow line, now it blotted out the brilliant glow of the glaciers, and now having climbed almost four miles it left the peak of Kilimanjaro in darkness, just a pale grey ghost against a blue-black sky.

24

Fall of Blackbeard

ROGER tried to sleep.

He soon gave it up as a bad job. The seat was uncomfortable. He would be better off on the ground.

He climbed down and stretched out on the grass under the remaining wing. He depended upon the wing to scare off any inquisitive animals. It was so low that no rhino, elephant, buffalo, or hippo could get under it.

But he had forgotten about another dangerous wild animal. The ant.

News of his presence spread to the occupants of the ant-hill against which the plane had crashed. He woke up with a start when he felt some sharp nips on his arms and legs. Before he could get fully awake the nips had spread under his clothes over his entire body and he was one trembling jelly of pain.

He leaped to his feet, tore off his clothes, danced and brushed and slapped and for every ant he got rid of two others arrived. His audience of animals looked on in amazement.

Then one of them came to his aid. It was really not at all interested in aiding him, but just in getting a good meal.

The ant-bear known also as the aardvark (meaning earth pig) cannot pass up a chance to dine on ants. It sleeps all day. At nightfall it wakes and goes out hungrily searching for food.

It is a beast about four feet in length, weighs something like one hundred and forty pounds, has bear-like claws for digging, a tail like a kangaroo's, long pointed ears that shoot off in different directions like those of a

donkey, a snout like a pig's and – most amazing of all – a sticky tongue eighteen inches long.

Roger's visitor immediately began thrashing that remarkable tongue into the army of ants that streamed from the ant-hill to Roger's trembling hide. The tongue, loaded with ants, was flicked back into the mouth, and down went the wriggling insects into the animal's paunch. Out darted the glue-covered ribbon to get a new load.

The ant has an intelligence far greater than one would expect in so small a creature, and the marching column promptly turned about and tried to escape into the ant-hill. But there were still numerous ants feasting upon Roger. Suddenly he felt a light stroke up his leg. The ant-bear was quite accustomed to tongueing ants from the hides of other animals. And to this bear Roger was just another beast, a table spread with food.

The boy stood perfectly still in order not to frighten his rescuer, and let the sticky, tickling tongue caress his hide. The moon must have laughed as it looked down on the strange spectacle. Roger himself laughed, as the tongue tickled, and at once the ant-bear took fright and clumsily galloped off.

Roger dressed and decided to spend the rest of the night in the co-pilot's seat, no matter how uncomfortable.

The ant-bear had one more surprise to give Roger. It stopped short as it saw a lion approaching. The ant-bear is a favourite food of the lion.

The lion also stopped. He was in no hurry. Being just a big cat, he acted like other cats. A cat chasing a mouse does not pounce upon it and eat it at once. It plays with it, turns its head away, pretends to take no interest in it, keeps it worrying for a while before finishing it off.

So the lion dilly-dallied, evidently sure that his victim could not escape. It's true, the ant-bear cannot run as fast as the lion. But the ant-bear is a powerful beast in its own way, equipped with strong curved claws with which it can dig a hole and vanish from sight within one minute.

And so, while the lion gazed off into space and

thought about the good meal he was about to have, the ant-bear silently and swiftly scooped away the earth. When the lion looked back the bagful of ants had disappeared and nothing was left but a hole.

The lion walked over to it, looked down into it, scratched at it and then walked off with a disappointed grumble.

Roger slept fitfully. Twice he was roused by the peculiar laugh of hyenas under the plane, probably nibbling at the tyres. He scared them away by stamping on the cabin floor. Then he slept soundly, undisturbed even by the squawling *Peeyah! Peeyah! Peeyah! Wah-wah!* of the bush-baby, so named because its cry is much like that of a very bad-tempered child.

He dreamed that he was being gored by the horns of a rhino, and woke to find that it was dawn and Hal was prodding him in the ribs.

'Come alive,' said his brother. 'Are you going to sleep all day? Here's your sandwich.'

With difficulty Roger got his eyes open and saw that with Hal was Warden Crosby, and behind them all the safari men and the cars.

'Pile out,' Hal said. 'We're on our way to the poachers' camp.'

'How about the plane?'

'Just have to leave it here. The warden telegraphed the Nairobi airport for mechanics. Let's get going and see what's under those brush mats.'

It was a little over twenty miles back to the grove of big-bellied hippo trees and the suspicious-looking mats.

Not a soul was to be seen. But the muffled sound of

voices came over the morning air.

If the pits were really full of poachers they would be armed with bows and arrows.

'Just raise one corner of this mat so that we can get a look,' Hal said.

The men lifted the corner of the brush roof. Hal peered down, half expecting to get an arrow in his face. There was no one in the pit.

And still there was that sound of voices.

The other pits were examined, one by one. There were animals in a few, but no humans.

Hal hushed his men. 'Keep quiet and listen.'

There was no doubt about it. Somewhere men were talking. The sound seemed to come from the trees. But there were no men among the baobabs. They could not be concealed by foliage, for there was no foliage – the trees were bare.

Hal led the way back among the trees. Again he hushed his men. But now there was no sound of talking. Nothing but a breathless silence. Either there were no poachers here or they had become aware that they were having visitors. Hal looked under the trees, behind the trees, up into the branches. Not a soul. Hal was ready to give it up as a bad job.

'Wait,' the warden said. 'They could be right here – all round us.'

'How could they be here without our seeing them?'

'You notice how big these tree-trunks are. The baobab doesn't grow more than about fifty feet high – but it grows sideways. Like a short fat man, a "five-by-five". Many of these trees have a waist measurement of sixty feet. That's a pretty big tummy. They are old trees –

anything from five hundred to a thousand years old. Now the peculiar thing about an old baobab is that it gets hollow. Any one of these trees could hold twenty men.'

'But how would they get in and out? I see no holes.'

'The opening is usually up there where the tree branches, about twelve feet above the ground.'

'Joro,' Hal said. 'Stand close to this trunk. Give me a hand up.'

He mounted to Joro's shoulders. There he could just reach the lowest branches. He pulled himself up. Now he could see the hole, just where the branches radiated from the trunk.

He crept to the edge of the hole, very cautiously so as not to invite a shower of arrows. He looked down into the gloom. The trunk was full of men. They stared up at him solemnly but made no move to attack him. They acted more like small boys who have been caught doing something naughty.

He drew back as the poachers began climbing out of the hole and dropping to the ground. They left their weapons behind them. Hal came down. Why weren't the poachers prepared to fight?

'Joro, ask them what this is all about.'

Joro spoke in Swahili. When one of the poachers replied Joro translated.

'They don't want to fight. They give up.'

'Why?'

'Every time they try to make a camp, we spoil it. They are tired of following Blackbeard. He isn't paying them – because he's getting no trophies. They say if they're not paid they won't work.'

Men were now pouring out of the other trees. Among the last was Blackbeard himself. But he was not ready to surrender. He carried a revolver in each hand, his beard bristled, and his face was contorted with rage. He screamed at his men, urging them to fight. He acted as if he had gone stark staring mad. He fired shots into the air, and when that did not terrify his men he levelled his guns upon them and blasted away at them, killing six.

Now the poachers were really stirred into action – against their own leader. They rushed him, losing two more men to his bullets before they pinned him to the earth and took away his guns. They might have killed him if the warden had not stopped them.

'Get up,' commanded the warden. Blackbeard, still blustering, rose to his feet.

Chee, who had come along with the safari men, was acting strangely. He sniffed at Blackbeard, then bared his teeth in a savage growl. Why, wondered Hal, should the cheetah behave so towards a man he had never seen or smelled before?

Blackbeard viciously kicked the cheetah in the throat. Hal remembered someone else who had attacked the animal in exactly the same way – Judge Singh.

Chee lunged at Blackbeard but was checked by his young master's voice. 'Stop it, Chee,' Roger commanded, fearing that in a fight between man and beast Chee himself might be killed.

The warden faced Blackbeard. 'Your game is up,' he said. 'We've been after you for years. Now we've got you – thanks to two boys.'

'There's nothing you can do to me,' said Blackbeard defiantly. 'I have money.'

'We'll see about that in court. You will stand trial for the murder of eight men. Sindar Singh himself will be your judge – and you will find him a pillar of justice. All your money cannot buy him off.'

Blackbeard broke into a loud laugh. At the sound, Chee leaped upon him. His teeth closed on the killer

king's throat. Not exactly on his throat, but on the beard that covered it.

The false beard came off in the animal's jaws.

And there, stripped of its disguise, was the face of Sindar Singh. Crosby gazed at it in amazement.

Judge Singh was still laughing. 'Now you see why I am not afraid of your Judge Singh,' he said. 'Ha, ha – it is really too funny. What a fool you have been.'

He changed his tune when he was bound hand and foot, transported to Nairobi, and delivered to the police.

There Singh alias Blackbeard did his best to buy off the judge who was to try him. He failed. When he was sentenced to life imprisonment he realized that not all judges were as corruptible as Judge Sindar Singh.

His wealth was confiscated and turned over to the African Wildlife Society to be devoted to the protection of African animals.

So the boys had been right – and wrong. They had guessed Singh was a crook. They had not guessed he was Blackbeard himself.

As for Warden Mark Crosby, the discovery that the soft-voiced little Judge Singh and the killer Blackbeard were one and the same person was a shock he would never quite get over. He had been fond of Singh. He was still fond of what Singh had seemed to be. He mourned the loss of a friend.

25

Man-eaters

THE morning after the capture of Blackbeard, a ranger brought the boys a note from Crosby.

'Would you drop over to my office? Urgent.'

When they entered the warden's banda they saw that he already had a visitor, a black man in the uniform of a railway official.

Crosby introduced him as Gazi Tanga, station master at near-by Mtito Andei where the Nairobi–Mombasa railway cuts through Tsavo Park.

'Tanga brings serious news,' said Crosby 'Last night five of his men were killed and eaten by lions.'

The boys were goggle-eyed. 'I thought man-eating lions were a thing of the past,' Hal said.

'Far from it. Every year more than a hundred people are killed by man-eaters in East Africa. Of course that isn't many, compared with those killed by cars in your country. But if lions kill the Africans the Africans are going to kill the lions. Now we want to protect both the people and the lions. Tanga's men are out this very morning killing every lion they can find. We can't allow that. The lions – the innocent ones – have a right to live. Visitors come from all over the world to see our lions. We can't have them wiped out. Most lions are peaceable. There are just a few bad actors. The thing to do is to find the bad actors and leave the good lions alone.'

'How can you tell by looking at a lion whether he is good or bad?'

'It isn't easy. That's why I called you in.'

'But we've had no experience in this sort of thing.'

'Perhaps not just this. But you've had a lot of experience with animals. And you seem to be good at solving riddles. You've done so much for me that I can't ask you to do anything more. But if you volunteer...'

He looked so hopeful that it was hard to refuse. Hal looked at Roger. Roger nodded.

'Of course we'll do what we can,' Hal said. 'We're lucky to have a good crew. Being Africans themselves, they know more about African animals than we could learn in a lifetime.'

'That may be so,' admitted the warden. 'But they're not inclined to do much about it. Put their know-how along with your energy and I believe you'll get somewhere.'

Hal turned to Tanga. 'What do you think? Perhaps you feel we cannot help you.'

'It is not so, bwana,' replied Tanga respectfully. 'We know you stopped poaching in Tsavo. We know you caught Blackbeard. It is all we need to know. We will do as you say.'

'Good. Then go back and tell your people to kill no

more lions. We will come with our crew in an hour. With your help we'll catch those bad actors.'

And how they failed – and succeeded – is told in another book, *Lion adventure.*

Willard Price 'Adventure' stories are all about Hal and Roger and their amazing adventures in search of wild animals for the world's zoos. Here is a complete list of the adventures available in Knight:

1 AMAZON ADVENTURE
2 SOUTH SEA ADVENTURE
3 UNDERWATER ADVENTURE
4 VOLCANO ADVENTURE
5 WHALE ADVENTURE
6 AFRICAN ADVENTURE
7 ELEPHANT ADVENTURE
8 SAFARI ADVENTURE
9 LION ADVENTURE
10 GORILLA ADVENTURE
11 DIVING ADVENTURE
12 CANNIBAL ADVENTURE
13 TIGER ADVENTURE
14 ARCTIC ADVENTURE

FALCON TRAVIS

PUZZLE TIME

This book contains a collection of over seventy ingenious and absorbing puzzles for you to pit your wits against. Many are specially designed to test your word power; others will challenge your general knowledge or your skill with numbers and all will provide you with brain-teasing fun.

KNIGHT BOOKS